PARLIAMENT
FOR EUROPE

by the same author

RAMSAY MACDONALD

DAVID MARQUAND

PARLIAMENT
FOR
EUROPE

JONATHAN CAPE
THIRTY BEDFORD SQUARE LONDON

First published 1979
Copyright © 1979 by David Marquand

Jonathan Cape Ltd, 30 Bedford Square, London WC1

British Library Cataloguing in Publication Data

Marquand, David
Parliament for Europe.
1. European Economic Community
2. European Coal and Steel Community
3. Euratom
382'.9142   HC241.2
ISBN 0–224–01716–0
ISBN 0–224–01717–9 Pbk

Printed in Great Britain
by Ebenezer Baylis & Son Ltd
The Trinity Press, Worcester, and London

Contents

Preface

A vast literature on the European Community already exists; I am uneasily aware that adding to it is a rash, even foolhardy, enterprise, not to be indulged in without good reason. I should therefore explain how this book came to be written and what its purpose is.

It is based on the best part of two years' experience as an official of the European Commission, and on many years' experience as a pro-European Labour M.P. I went to Brussels as a committed supporter of the European Community and of the ideal of European integration: I came back even more strongly committed than when I had left. But although I still believe — if possible, more firmly than before — that the European Community is the single most hopeful political experiment of our time, my experience in Brussels led me to the conclusion that the Community's present institutional arrangements are dangerously ill-adapted to its needs, and that there is a serious possibility that the experiment will fail if those arrangements are not changed. I also came to the conclusion that the prevailing British view of the nature and purpose of the Community is mistaken, and that Britain will not be able to play a satisfactory part in Community affairs until that view is abandoned. It is that double case that I argue in what follows.

Accordingly, this book is intended to be prescriptive rather than descriptive: a tract rather than a treatise. I have included as much factual material as I thought necessary to illuminate my theme and support my argument, but I am less concerned to describe the Community as it is than to propose the changes which I believe to be needed if the Community is to become what I think it ought to be. In the note on further reading at the end, I list a number of analytical studies of various aspects of the Community's history and structure, as well as some introductory surveys, designed for readers unfamiliar with the subject. This book belongs to a different category, and should be judged by different criteria.

The author of even a small book incurs a frighteningly large number of debts. Some of the ideas put forward here were first explored, in a rather different form, in an article in *Political Quarterly*. I am greatly indebted for comments on this article to Professor Ghita Ionescu, Mr Robert Jackson, Mrs Helen Wallace, Mr William Wallace and to a number of former colleagues on the staff of the European Commission and the European Parliament; needless to say, all errors of fact and interpretation are my own.

I should also like to thank Mrs Jill Sutcliffe, of Jonathan Cape, for the devoted vigilance she brought to the task of editing, and my secretary, Mrs Pat Bellotti, for the energy and enthusiasm with which she typed successive drafts of the manuscript, often in very difficult circumstances. But for her, and Miss Ruth Fingerhut, who also helped with the typing, the manuscript would never have got to the printer in time.

Last, but by no means least, I should like to thank my wife, Judith, for her encouragement and support, as well as for the fortitude with which she bore the experience of author's widowhood while carrying out a double move of house.

Buxworth   D.M.
January 1979

I

Pragmatism is not Enough

In July 1979 a directly elected Parliament, representing almost 200 million voters in the nine member states of the European Community, will meet for the first time. It will be a unique institution. International parliamentary assemblies, with members drawn from the Parliaments of a range of sovereign states, associated together for some common purpose, have been familiar features of the political landscape for some time. The Council of Europe has such an assembly, the members of which are drawn from the Parliaments of the 19 countries which belong to the Council of Europe. There is a NATO Assembly, with members drawn from the Parliaments of the 15 NATO countries. The Inter-Parliamentary Union and the Commonwealth Parliamentary Association hold regular gatherings, at which parliamentarians from all the Parliaments which belong to those bodies meet and discuss problems of common concern. Until now, the European Parliament has been a body of the same sort. Its members, too, have been drawn from the national Parliaments of the member states of the European Community. Though many of them have devoted a great deal of energy and time to Community affairs, they have been able to sit in the European Parliament only because they were first elected to a national Parliament, to represent a national constituency. But the European Parliament which is to be elected this summer will be a quite different animal. It will not be an international Assembly, but a supra- or, at any rate, a trans-national one. Though many of its members will also belong to a national Parliament, they will not sit in it by virtue of their membership of a national Parliament. Each will have a Community mandate and represent a Community constituency. Together, they — and they alone—will be able to speak in the name of the people of the Community as a whole, in a sense which has been true of no one until now.

The directly elected European Parliament will have few formal powers—so few that some commentators have argued that it ought not to be described as a 'Parliament' at all.[1] But it will have considerable moral authority. More important still, the elections from which it will spring will provide an opportunity for political parties and ordinary voters to express their views about the future development of the Community in a way which has not been open to them in the past. For although Community decision-makers have always been highly sensitive to the wishes of organised interest groups, both at the national and at the Community level, the voter *qua* voter has hardly been involved in the decision-making process. National elections are fought on national issues: Community issues figure only marginally, if at all. The national Governments, whose representatives in the Council of Ministers have the last word in Community decisions, are, of course, acutely conscious of the possible repercussions on their domestic political fortunes of the positions they adopt in Luxembourg or Brussels. But they do not have to formulate a Community policy and justify that policy to an electorate. Thus the Community's decision-making process violates one of the central elements in the liberal-democratic political creed to which all nine of the Community's Governments pay lip-service. In a democracy, the people are supposed to be able to choose between alternative policies, submitted to them by rival political leaders or groups of leaders. A large range of decisions, which impinge in a whole variety of ways on the lives of ordinary people throughout the Community, are now taken at Community level. But the people have no opportunity to choose between alternative Community policies, while the political leaders have no incentive to frame them.

Hitherto, members of the European Parliament have been in the same position as national ministers. They too have been returned to national Parliaments in national elections; for all practical purposes, their constituents have been powerless either to reward or to punish them for their actions at the European level. Of course, the elections to the new European Parliament may also be fought, in practice, on national issues. But it will, at least, be possible to fight them on Community issues; and, to put it at its lowest, the parties which contest them will look rather foolish if they say nothing about such issues at all. In any case, elections are not the exclusive property of the politicians who fight them. The media play important roles as well. So, for that matter, do the voters. Some of the politicians seeking election to the European Parliament may try to conceal their true views on the issues facing the Community. Given reasonable skill on the part of the media, and reasonable assiduity on the part of even a comparatively small number of electors, they can be forced, if not to come clean, then at least to behave less grubbily than they would like.

'Can', however, not 'will'. The elections will give voters and political parties an opportunity to express their views about the future development of the Community. They carry no guarantee that the opportunity will be taken. The elections will be fought on Community issues only if those who fight them are aware of the real choices now facing the Community, and are prepared to define their attitudes to those choices. It is of the utmost importance that they should do so. There is a great deal of urgent business to transact at Community level in the next few years. To name only a few matters, Community decision-makers will have, between now and 1984, to determine the shape of a Community energy policy, to decide what response the Community should make to the competition it is meeting from newly-industrialising countries from the Philippines to Brazil, to decide whether and if so how the common agricultural policy should be reshaped to take account of the needs of the southern European applicants for Community membership, and to devise a more equitable Community Budget which gives greater benefits to the poorer member states. On all these matters, Community voters—in Britain at least as much as in the other member states—have a right to know what their politicians think. Yet in Britain remarkably few politicians seem to be aware of the choices facing the Community in these fields, and fewer still seem to be prepared to define their attitudes to them. Now that the dust is settling, it is clear that

3

three schools of thought were engaged in the battle over British entry into the Community, not two. It is also clear that the school to which most policy-makers belonged, and which had most influence on the final outcome, understood least well what the Community was for and what membership of it would entail. Finally, it is clear that that school of thought still predominates in both major parties and in most of Whitehall.

Integrationists and Anti-integrationists

At one end of the spectrum of opinion were the convinced supporters of European integration, who agreed with Jean Monnet that the Community's objective was not merely to 'coalesce states' but to 'unite men',[2] and who wished to join it for that reason. Some of these were also federalists, who looked forward to the creation of a United States of Europe, modelled, more or less exactly, on the United States of America. Others agreed with Edward Heath that it was unnecessary, and perhaps even undesirable, to devise a precise blueprint for eventual European political union and that it was wiser, as he put it in his remarkable 1967 Godkin Lectures, 'to define a political community in terms of the content of its decisions: that is, to say that a European political community comes into being when most of the decisions which are the stuff of political debate in any one country are taken on a Community basis'.[3] All integrationists, however, believed that the classical European nation state was no longer capable of safeguarding the interests of its citizens and that it was necessary, in some sense or other, to transcend it. They did not always approve of the way in which the Community of Six had set about the task. But for all of them, the supranational element in the Community structure was a positive attraction, and membership of a supranational community a positive goal.

At the other end were the convinced opponents of integration. Most of these agreed that the Community was in the business of transcending the national state. Some, though probably a minority, saw no objection to its doing so. But all believed that Britain should refuse to take part in that business.

4

Membership of a supranational Community might or might not be a good thing for the continentals who had set it up. It would be a thoroughly bad thing for Britain. There were, of course, different opinions as to why it would be a bad thing for Britain. Right-wing opponents of integration were apt to suggest that there was some special quality in the British nation state, or perhaps in the British people, which made membership of a supranational Community impossible for it. The British were 'offshore islanders', not continentals; their national genius would be outraged if they were dragooned into membership of a continental Community. The British Parliament was sovereign in a sense true of no other Parliament, and it was inherently unable to relinquish its sovereignty in the way that membership of a supranational Community would entail. Some left-wing anti-integrationists, on the other hand, agreed with the integrationists that the classical nation state had had its day, or at any rate said that they agreed with them. For this group, the Community was objectionable, not because it was supranational but because it was supranational in the wrong way. They would have liked nothing better, they insisted, than to join a socialist, 'outward-looking', supranational Community. What they refused to do was to join a capitalist, 'inward-looking' one.[4]

These differences were, however, more apparent than real. On two central propositions, right-wing and left-wing anti-integrationists were agreed. The first was that Britain was a different kind of country from her continental neighbours. For right-wing anti-integrationists the difference lay, above all, in the special characteristics of the British genius, the British character and the British state. For their left-wing bed-fellows, it lay in the fact that, whereas the continental countries which had entered the Community were irredeemably capitalist, Britain on her own might find her way to Socialism. The second proposition was that, whatever might be true of the continental nation states, the British nation state *was* still capable of safeguarding the interests of its citizens, or at any rate could become so under the right kind of leadership. Right-wing anti-integrationists thought it should come from the right and left wing anti-integrationists that it should come from the left. But they all agreed that it could come from somewhere, and that once it

5

came, the British nation state would put the troubles of the recent past behind it and enjoy a rebirth of power, or moral influence, or both. Entry into a supranational Community would therefore be a kind of treachery, for it would make such a rebirth impossible for ever.

The anti-integrationists touched some powerful chords. It is, after all, true that Britain is an offshore island, whose traditions and political culture are different from those of her continental neighbours. It is not a little matter that Britain was never ruled by Napoleon, had no revolution in 1848 and was unoccupied in the Second World War. Still less is it a little matter that the most powerful tribal symbols of the British—Drake chasing the Spaniards up the Channel, Nelson in Hardy's arms at Trafalgar, Wellington encouraging his men to withstand the hard pounding at Waterloo, the Few fighting off the Luftwaffe in 1940—evoke memories of military victories over an encroaching continental system. The British are not the only people in Europe with what Hugh Gaitskell once referred to as a thousand years of history. Indeed, the *British* have much less than a thousand years of history. Scotland was an independent Kingdom until the Act of Union in 1707, and Britain is therefore a parvenu compared, not only to France, but to Denmark and the Netherlands among the existing member-states of the Community, and to Spain and Portugal among the latest applicants for membership. Even the English cannot boast older or more stirring symbols than the French. Joan of Arc is at least as impressive a figure as Henry V; except to the eye of love, Charlemagne surely outguns Alfred the Great. But although French nationalism is as tenacious and deep-rooted as English or British nationalism, its emotional relationship with the rest of Europe is quite different. Frenchmen have often tried to dominate Europe. No Frenchman has doubted that he was a European. A Frenchman's thousand years of history would be a thousand years of inextricable involvement with the rest of the continent. Gaitskell's was meant to symbolise, and to his audience almost certainly did symbolise, a history of escape from continental entanglements. It was a mythical escape, of course. In reality, Britain has always been as inextricably bound up with the rest of Europe as France and Germany;

6

like theirs, her security has always depended, in the last resort, on the ability of her soldiers to win battles against other Europeans on the European land-mass.[5] But we are dealing here with myths, not realities; and the myth of the Open Sea is one of the most powerful in the British political culture. It was a potent ally for the anti-integrationists.

The Pragmatic View

The behaviour of the third school of thought which was engaged in the struggle over British entry into the Community can be understood only against this background. These were the pragmatists — for whom the integrationists' vision of a supranational Community transcending the nation state, and the anti-integrationists' vision of the Island Race turning its back on the continent, were equally repellent. At first, the pragmatists assumed that the Community would fail, and therefore refused to think seriously about whether to join or not. By the end of the 1950s, however, doubts were beginning to creep in. It was clear that the Economic Community set up by the 1957 Rome Treaty was succeeding after all, and that, as Harold Macmillan put it, 'the major continental powers are united in a positive economic grouping, with considerable political aspects, which ... may have the effect of excluding us both from European markets and from consultation in European Policy'.[6] If a new power *bloc* was growing up on Britain's doorstep, and if Britain was unable to stop it from growing up, *Realpolitik* suggested that the only safe course was to join it; and by the early 1960s the pragmatists had become convinced by this reasoning. But although they came to share the integrationists' view that Britain could no longer safeguard her interests satisfactorily outside the Community, and reached the integrationists' conclusion that she should therefore join the Community, they had reached it by a quite different route. The integrationists wanted to join the Community because they wanted to transcend the nation state. The pragmatists wanted to do so because they thought that Britain would have a better chance of influencing world affairs as one of a group of sovereign

7

states than as a single sovereign state on her own. The point of joining was to maximise the power of the sovereign British state, not to help create a new kind of political entity, none of whose members would be sovereign states in the traditional sense.

They knew, of course, that the Community's founders had said that it would develop along supranational lines, that there were supranational elements in its constitution and that many of those active in its affairs continued to use the language of supranationalism. But they dismissed all that as window-dressing. It was the kind of thing in which continentals, with their strange interest in first principles and their even stranger habit of pretending that practical conclusions should be deduced from first principles, could be expected to indulge. It was not the kind of thing about which serious British politicians needed to worry their heads. For in spite of the supranational talk emanating from Brussels, the supranational elements in the Community's constitution were of little practical importance. De Gaulle had cut the Commission down to size, and the European Parliament had never amounted to anything anyway. The institution that mattered was the Council of Ministers, in which each member government had a veto. Membership of the Community would, of course, lessen Britain's freedom of action. But so did membership of NATO or even membership of the United Nations. The differences between NATO and the Community — the fact that there is no NATO institution remotely analogous to the Commission or the European Court, for example, or the fact that the Treaty setting up the Community explicitly states that its object is an 'ever-closer union', clearly implying that it is intended to embrace more fields of activity in the future than it did at the outset — were of no significance. The Community's true objective, the pragmatists told themselves, was precisely to 'coalesce states'. It was an association of sovereign nations, working together for certain purposes but not others, and reaching its decisions by the familiar processes of intergovernmental horse-trading — differing from NATO in the subject matters with which it was concerned, but belonging to the same ancient and unalarming political species.

That was what it was, and that was also what it would

remain. Some pragmatists sometimes insisted that they did not wish to pre-empt or even to forecast the future: that the citizens of the Community might one day decide that they wanted it to be significantly more supranational than it was at present, and that such a decision might be right. In a speech at the Guildhall at the apogee of his Europeanism, in the summer of 1969, Harold Wilson implied that, although a supranational Community was, of course, out of the question for the moment, it might become a possibility in ten or twenty years' time.[7] But that was not the general view. Much more common was the attitude expressed by David Owen, when he declared that although 'federalism' was a 'noble goal', it was 'for most of us in Britain unrealistic and to some mythical ... In the main the British outlook is practical. We cannot see in concrete terms how nine nations with very different political, social and cultural traditions — some of them young nations in European terms — can possibly be federated over any time-scale of political activity on which it is realistic to focus.'[8]

Dr Owen's was, no doubt, a muddled attitude, and at the same time a patronising one. Why should it be more difficult to federate 'young' nations than old ones? Which 'young' nations resist 'federalism', and why should their resistance rule it out? In what conceivable sense were such enthusiastic supranationalists as Jean Monnet or Robert Schuman, say, less 'practical' than the British ministers and officials who took it for granted that the E.E.C. would come to nothing and concluded that there was no need for Britain to take it seriously? But it was also a characteristic attitude. Many pragmatists were as moved as most integrationists were by the spectacle of an ancient continent healing the wounds which it had inflicted on itself in the past. Most were as anxious that Europe should unite. But they meant something different by unity. For them, even more than for the anti-integrationists, the nation state was irreducible. It was possible for a group of nation states to stand together in their dealings with the outside world, to follow common policies in some fields and to align their policies in others, to allow each other's goods and services to be exchanged freely across their frontiers — to take, in short, all and perhaps even more than all the practical steps which the signatories of the Rome Treaty had bound themselves to take. It was not possible to transcend the nation state altogether, to create a Community in which, to use Mr Heath's formula, 'most of the decisions which are the stuff of political debate in any one country' would be taken on a Community rather than on a national basis. To suggest that it was possible would be to arouse fears which had no foundation and hopes which could never be realised. And to do that would be to do the Community more harm than good.

Why Britain joined

Integrationists played important parts in the arguments that led the Macmillan Government to apply for membership in 1961, and that led the Wilson government to renew the application in 1967. Without the votes of integrationist Labour M.P.s in 1971, and the abstentions of a much smaller number of integrationist Labour M.P.s during the passage of the European Communities Bill in 1972, the Heath Government could not have taken Britain into the Community in the end. Mr Heath himself was clearly an integrationist; so was Roy Jenkins; so, rather less clearly, perhaps, was Lord George-Brown. Some of the officials most closely concerned with the decisions of successive governments to apply for membership, and with the negotiations of the early 1960s and early 1970s, were integrationists as well, or became integrationists when they looked at the evidence. The Liberal Party had been committed to membership since the mid-1950s, largely on integrationist grounds: and there were some integrationists on the back benches in both major parties at an early stage in the argument. But although Britain would not have joined the Community without the integrationists, there can be little doubt that it was the pragmatic arguments, not the integrationist ones, which persuaded both the Conservative Government in 1960–1 and the Labour Government in 1966–7 that Britain had no alternative but to join the Community.

Harold Macmillan had been a supporter of European unity in the late 1940s, but he had not taken an integrationist line in the arguments that divided pro-Europeans at that time; in 1950 he had roundly declared *à propos* of the Schuman Plan that, 'Our people will not hand over to any supranational authority the right to close down our pits and our steelworks'.[9] He had been Foreign Secretary when the Six were laying the foundations of the Rome Treaty and was therefore ministerially responsible for the decision that Britain should be represented at their discussions only by a medium-rank official, with no authority to commit the Government, rather than by a Minister with full negotiating status. Though his memoirs are understandably coy on the question it seems clear that he was so far removed from the integrationist position in the middle 1950s as to share the common Whitehall view that there was no chance that an Economic Community would come into existence on the European continent, and that in any case Britain's non-European ties, with the United States and the Commonwealth, were of much greater value to her than her links with Europe. It seems equally clear that he changed his mind about the desirability of joining the Community in the late 1950s or at the beginning of the 1960s for hard pragmatic reasons. The failure of the Suez Expedition in 1956 and of his own diplomacy in 1959 and 1960 had taught him that Britain was no longer a world power in a sense not true of France or Germany. The special relationship with Washington was growing less special as time went on; in any event, the Americans were alarmed by the possibility that a rift between the British-dominated European Free Trade Area and the Community of the Six might weaken the West in the face of the Soviet threat, and were therefore anxious for Britain to join the Community. In spite of early British scepticism, the Community was developing rapidly, and seemed likely to pose a threat to Britain's economic and political interests unless the British Government were in a position to influence its decisions.

Such considerations could, no doubt, have led equally well to an integrationist conclusion: the line between pragmatists, who came reluctantly to believe that since Britain could not stop the Six from creating a new continental power *bloc* she had better join them, and integrationists, who argued that since no European nation state could any longer safeguard the interests of its citizens it was necessary to transcend the limitations of traditional statehood in a supranational Community, was not hard and fast. But although it would have been perfectly logical for Macmillan to reach an integrationist conclusion, there is no evidence — either in his memoirs, in the memoirs of his Cabinet colleagues at the time or in the contemporary public record — that he in fact did so. On the contrary, the available evidence strongly suggests that he did not: that he wanted to join the Community because he wanted to retain as much power in the hands of the British state as he could, and because he believed that this could be done better inside than outside. And if this was true of Macmillan it was more obviously true of Butler, Maudling and Home — central figures in the Conservative Government at the time, who could undoubtedly have prevented a British application for membership had they wished to do so.

It was the same with the Labour Government, only more so. Roy Jenkins and George Brown had been strongly in favour of British membership of the Community, in Jenkins's case, at any rate on integrationist grounds, while their party was in opposition. They stuck to their guns when they entered office. But although Jenkins was a commanding figure during his term as Chancellor of the Exchequer, he did not arrive at the Treasury until after De Gaulle's second veto. Brown, as Secretary of Economic Affairs from 1964 to 1966, and even more as Foreign Secretary from 1966 to 1968, played a more important role, but he could not have pushed the Government into renewing the Conservative application without the support of less committed figures. All the evidence suggests that these less committed figures were swayed by the same pragmatic arguments which had swayed their Conservative equivalents a few years before.

Chief among them was Harold Wilson. Unlike Macmillan, Wilson had no European 'past'; though he had not opposed British entry to the Community on principle in the arguments over the Conservative application from 1961 to 1963, he had been distinctly lukewarm about it. Yet within a couple of years of arriving in No. 10, he had swung round to vigorous, even passionate, support. Like Macmillan's, his memoirs are silent on the reasons for his conversion. As with Macmillan's, however, they are not hard to guess. Wilson had arrived at No. 10 as an instinctive Atlanticist, believing that Britain's ties with the United States were far more important to her than her ties with Europe, and with an almost Kiplingesque conception of her responsibilities as a world power. His long-drawn-out struggle to maintain the value of the pound taught him that the effective discharge of those responsibilities was beyond her economic strength; he also discovered that, in the era of Lyndon Johnson and the deepening American involvement in Vietnam, the special relationship with Washington, in so far as it existed, was a burden rather than an asset. But if the world role and the special relationship with Washington were to be abandoned, it seemed that the choice for Britain would lie, in the long term, between effective isolation and diminishing influence on world affairs on the one hand, and membership of the Community on the other.

Like Macmillan, however, Wilson did not draw an integrationist conclusion from his experience, although he could have done. For him, as for Macmillan, the point of joining the Community was to maintain Britain's power, not to subsume it in a supranational Europe: to find a new route to the 'top table', not to work out a new kind of seating plan, in which no European state would sit separately at any kind of table, top or bottom.[10] As with the Conservatives, the same seems to have been true of most of those pivotal figures, who swung from hostility to support for entry during Wilson's term of office, and without whose support Wilson and Brown could not have applied for membership in 1967. It is true that some former opponents of entry had swung right over to integrationism by the early 1970s — Lords Gordon-Walker and Thomson are obvious examples — and it is possible that they had done so by the mid-1960s. But such key figures as James Callaghan and Denis Healey were persuaded of the advantages of membership, in so far as they were persuaded at all, by the pragmatic arguments; to judge by their subsequent behaviour, at any rate, the same must be true of the lesser figures in the Cabinet as well.

That was the position in the 1960s and that has remained the position in the 1970s. It is true that the driving force which kept the Conservatives committed to entry was provided, above all by Edward Heath, and that Mr Heath was the most articulate integrationist among senior British politicians. It is also true that, but for Roy Jenkins's refusal to abandon his commitment to entry, there would not have been enough support on the Labour benches to get the terms agreed upon in Brussels and Luxembourg through the House of Commons, and that Roy Jenkins was an integrationist as well. But it is doubtful if there were many integrationists in Mr Heath's Cabinet, and clear that there were very few in the Labour Cabinet which 'renegotiated' the terms of Britain's membership between 1974 and 1975, and then advised acceptance of the results of the 'renegotiations' to the British people in the 1975 referendum. It is clearer still that membership was recommended to the public, both by the Heath Government in 1971 and 1972, and by the Wilson Government in 1975, almost wholly in pragmatic terms. It was the opponents of entry who dilated on the supranational character of the Community, and pointed out that Britain's 'sovereignty' would be impaired if she went in. Supporters did their best to focus the debate on other matters — chiefly on the long-term 'dynamic' effects of entry on the British economy, and on the political and economic costs of staying out. When forced to discuss the question of sovereignty, they pointed reassuringly to the veto, thus implying that the Community was not really supranational after all, or talked vaguely about the need for Britain to 'pool' her sovereignty with those of her Community partners, thus implying that in some strange way she would have more sovereignty in than out. Few put the case for transcending sovereignty and joining an avowedly supranational Community, the whole *raison d'être* of which was that it was supranational.

The pragmatic view of the nature and purposes of the Community is still the prevailing British view. It provided the intellectual underpinning for the 'compromesso storico' between the pro- and anti-market wings of the Labour Party, which was set out in the Prime Minister's letter to the General Secretary, Mr Hayward, in the autumn of 1977, and which, in effect, committed the Party to support continued membership of the Community provided the Community did not develop in a supranational direction. It determined Labour's line in the debates within the Confederation of Socialist Parties about a

14

possible Confederation manifesto for the elections to the European Parliament. It has been repeated again and again by the
Foreign Secretary; and it permeated the speeches made by the
Home Office ministers in the parliamentary debates on the
European Assembly Bill in 1977 and 1978. It has been echoed
frequently by other ministers as well—even by ministers who,
in opposition, risked their political lives in the cause of European
unity.[11] Meanwhile, Opposition spokesmen have vied with each
other in attacking 'federalism' and, initially at least, reacted to
the monetary initiatives of Chancellor Schmidt and President
Giscard d'Estaing with a mixture of xenophobia and incompre-
hension almost worthy of Her Majesty's Treasury. All the
evidence suggests that the pragmatic view is as firmly entrenched in Whitehall, at any rate in the Home Departments,
as it is in Westminster; and it seems clear that it will continue
to be the view of the British Government whatever the result
of the next election. This consensus, moreover, is challenged
much more frequently by opponents of integration than by
supporters. A few battle-scarred veterans in the European
Movement still advocate more transfers of power from the
national to the Community level, but their voices are not very
loud and do not carry very far. In so far as a debate on Europe
is still going on in the United Kingdom, it is one in which the
anti-Europeans point in horror to the prospect of a supranational Community, while the pro-Europeans insist, with a
kind of knowing blandness, that no such prospect exists.

The Community since the Treaty

At first sight, the pragmatists seem to have history on their side.
No one can pretend that the Community has transcended the
nation state. In so far as it has 'united men' rather than 'coalesc-
ing states', it has done so only negatively. For economic integration has two faces, which can be described respectively as
negative and positive. Negative integration, to use the terminology of one of the leading authorities in the field, entails
'the removal of discrimination as between the economic agents
of the member countries'. Positive discrimination is much more

far-reaching. It consists of 'the formation and application of co-ordinated and common policies on a sufficient scale to ensure that major economic and welfare objectives are fulfilled'.[12] Negative integration is obviously much easier to achieve. It is not difficult to make precise treaty provisions for the removal of discrimination, and for the policing of its removal. It is much more difficult to define the content of a common policy in advance, and more difficult still to police a treaty obligation to frame a common policy. Partly because of this, and partly because there was a consensus in favour of negative integration among the Governments concerned, but no consensus in favour of positive integration, the Rome Treaty outlined the measures necessary for negative integration with great precision and detail, but referred to the measures which would be needed for positive integration only in general terms, if at all. The Community's activities were set out in Article Three. This bound the signatories to a number of fairly precise measures of negative integration, most of which were amplified in considerable detail in later articles – the elimination of tariffs and quantitative restrictions on trade between Member States, the establishment of a common external tariff, the abolition of obstacles to the free movement of persons, services and capital and the establishment of a 'system ensuring that competition in the Common Market is not distorted'. Article Three also contained some provisions for positive integration, laying it down that common policies were to be adopted for agriculture and transport, looking forward to the creation of a European Social Fund and a European Investment Bank, and declaring that one of the Community's activities should be 'the application of procedures by which the economic policies of the Member States can be co-ordinated and disequilibria in their balances of payments remedied'. But although the subsequent Title dealing with agriculture was fairly detailed, that dealing with transport was much vaguer, while the articles dealing with conjunctural policy were so general as to be virtually meaningless.

The Community's history since then has reflected the priorities set out in the Treaty. The customs union and the common external tariff were established much more quickly than had been expected. Though complete freedom of movement for persons, services and capital is still a long way off, many of the obstacles to it have been removed, and the Commission has made gallant efforts to persuade member Governments to remove others. Competition within the Common Market is by no means free of distortion, but an elaborate battery of regulations and directives has been created to prevent it. The Commission both has and uses the power to take Member Governments to court if this system of common rules is persistently violated; and the Court of Justice has consistently interpreted the relevant Treaty provisions in a maximalist fashion. Even negative integration is still incomplete, largely because of the substantive difficulty of harmonising professional qualifications across a continent, and because, in times of depression, protectionist pressures still make themselves felt at the national rather than at the Community level. It cannot yet be said that no Member State discriminates in favour of economic agents from among its own nationals and against those from other Community countries. But enormous progress has been made towards the goal of non-discrimination, and although the Council of Ministers often refuses to act on a Commission proposal in this field, few dispute that it is a legitimate field of Community activity.

The record on positive integration is very different. The most important form of positive integration so far achieved is the establishment of the common agricultural policy; and although the C.A.P. has been created in a way that runs counter to the national interests of the United Kingdom it is, by any reckoning, a remarkable achievement. Because of the special peculiarities of the farming industry, agricultural markets are, almost always, managed markets; and the creation of a managed Community market in place of a series of managed national markets clearly entails a much bigger transfer of power from the national to the Community level than is entailed by the mere removal of obstacles to free trade. Yet in spite of technical and political difficulties, a managed Community market in agricultural products was created surprisingly quickly, and it is still one of the most important elements in the so-called *acquis communautaire*. This achievement, however, dates from the early days of the Community. The crucial decisions of principle were taken more than seventeen years ago, and agreement on common cereal prices was reached in 1964. Since then, progress towards positive integration has been laggard or non-existent. In spite of the treaty provisions to the contrary, the Community still lacks a proper transport policy. The obligation to co-ordinate economic policies has been honoured in the breach much more frequently than in the observance. In spite of the patent inability of member Governments to restructure obsolescent and uncompetitive industries in the face of competition from newly-industrialising countries in Asia and South America, no coherent Community industrial policy has been created to supplement inadequate national policies. In spite of the commitment made at the Paris Summit in 1972, and the establishment of the Regional Development Fund and a Regional Policy Directorate General in the Commission, the Community's regional policy is still weak and ineffective, as is its social policy. The Community budget has grown in size and economic impact, but it still accounts for only 0.7 per cent of total Community G.N.P. It is, moreover, heavily weighted in favour of agriculture, which absorbs almost three-quarters of the appropriations. Energy, by contrast, accounts for only 0.4 per cent and regional policy for 4 per cent.

To make matters worse, the most significant 'positive' achievement of the early 1960s — the common agricultural policy—has almost been wrecked by the monetary divergences of the 1970s. The C.A.P. was supposed to achieve common prices, and a common market for agricultural produce, throughout the Community. As soon as community currencies started to fluctuate in value, the system was in jeopardy. Common prices have to be calculated in terms of a common accounting unit of some kind. If country A's currency appreciated in value against that common unit, the farmers of country A would receive less in terms of their own currency, irrespective of their efficiency or inefficiency, and if country B's depreciated, the farmers of country B would receive more. A system of 'Monetary Compensatory Amounts' was introduced to insulate farmers' incomes from the effects of currency changes, and it is only because of these that the C.A.P. has been kept afloat at all. But the M.C.A.s have only camouflaged the problem. They have not got rid of it; and they have introduced perverse side-effects of their own. The M.C.A. system means that, although common prices in units of amount exist on paper, they are not applied in the real world: there is a multi-tier price system with Britain at the bottom end of the range and Germany at the top. The net effect of the M.C.A. system, moreover, has been to subsidise the agricultural exports of the countries with appreciating currencies, with the result that the most expensive agricultural produce in the Community—namely, Germany's—receives a handsome export subsidy, and that the farmers who produce it are kept in business when in any rational system they would be encouraged to leave.

Meanwhile, the balance of institutional power has been changed, to the detriment of the supranational elements in the Community's construction, and to the advantage of the national authorities. The Rome Treaty was modelled on the Paris Treaty setting up the Coal and Steel Community, but it diverged in certain crucial respects from the model on which it was based. In the Coal and Steel Community, the High Authority was the decision-making body; the Council of Ministers could intervene only in specific cases. In the Economic Community, the Council was to take the decisions. The Commission was, however, supposed to provide the driving force in the system. The Council was to take decisions on proposals submitted to it by the Commission, so that although the Council would have the last word the Commission would have the first. Though it is always dangerous to infer political intentions from legal texts, it seems clear that the founders of the Community intended the dialogue between the Commission and the Council to be conducted on terms of near equality. It seems equally clear that they did not intend the Council to act as a forum for intergovernmental bargaining, but as a Community institution with an obligation to form a view of the general interest of the Community as a whole. After a transitional period, most Council decisions were to be taken by majority vote—by a simple majority on unimportant matters, and on important matters by a complicated system of weighted voting. This had the treble effect of ensuring that two large countries could not be outvoted by a coalition of one large country and three small ones; that no large country could block a proposal unless it were supported in its wish to do so by at least one other Member State; and that the three large countries could overrule the three small ones only if they were doing so in support of a Commission proposal. Commission proposals, moreover, could be amended by the Council only if the Council were unanimous.

The implications of this complicated structure cannot be examined in detail here, but two points should be noticed. In the first place, the Commission had more weight in the system than the simple statement that the power of decision lay with the Council might suggest. The Commission could get its proposals through Council, provided it had the support of the three large countries or, alternatively, of two large countries, together with Belgium and the Netherlands. Though its proposals could be thrown out altogether by any four Member States, they could not be watered down or twisted away from their original purposes against its will, unless all six Member States were agreed. Secondly, and much more importantly, each Member State, in agreeing to the concept of mandatory majority voting, had effectively declared in advance that, over a whole range of important matters, it would, if necessary, subordinate its own view of its national interest to a majority view of the Community interest. The same had been true of the Coal and Steel Community, of course, but the Coal and Steel Community covered a much narrower field than did the Economic Community. The signatories of the Rome Treaty had embarked on what has been well described as a 'journey to an unknown destination'.[13] In accepting the provisions for majority voting, they had committed themselves to take part in the journey even if they did not get their way about the route.

In the event, however, the provisions for majority voting never came properly into force. In the so-called 'Luxembourg Compromise' of 1966, France and the other five Member States agreed to disagree about President de Gaulle's demand that Member States should be allowed to insist on unanimity when they considered that matters of 'vital national importance' were being decided, even in areas where majority voting was envisaged in the Treaty. But the Compromise was a compromise only in name. In practice, the French got what they wanted; and in the nature of the case, this necessarily meant that the other Member States also got what the French wanted. After the Compromise, any Member State could insist on unanimity whenever it wished to do so, and all Council discussions — even on issues which were, in the end, settled by a majority — were conducted in the shadow of a possible veto. It is true, of course, that total intransigence does not pay in the Council of Ministers, any more than in any other committee. As the Germans discovered in the arguments over the site of the JET project, and as the French discovered in the struggle over whether the Commission should be represented at meetings of the 'Western Summit', the position of odd-man-out can sometimes be made so uncomfortable that a Government in a minority will sometimes lose more than it gains by sticking out against the majority. But this is true of all intergovernmental organisations, and indeed of all diplomacy. It does not alter the fact that the Luxembourg Compromise destroyed one of the central elements of the Treaty system. For the Treaty committed Member Governments to accept the result of a majority vote in the areas where majority voting was to be applied before they knew what the result would be, or even what proposal would be put forward. That crucial element of prior commitment has now disappeared; and, as the Vedel committee pointed out seven years ago, the result is that:

> The dose of innovation which could and normally should be included in [the Commission's] proposals is likely to be sacrificed in the search for solutions which will meet with unanimous approval ... [It] is clear that there is an increasing tendency for the Community decision-making process to consist of pure, diplomatic-style negotiations. This situation arises not so much from a failure to follow the Treaties as from the practical distortion of powers and institutions.[14]

It would be wrong to exaggerate. The 'negative' achievements mentioned above are immensely impressive when set against the preceding centuries of European history. However feeble they may be, the supranational elements in the Community's constitution exist, and refuse obstinately to disappear. In world affairs—as shown by its performance at the United Nations, in the North-South Conference in Paris and in the GATT multifibre negotiations—the Community has become a significant force, displaying considerable solidarity *vis-à-vis* other countries and gaining considerable tangible benefits for its members by doing so. The fact remains, however, that in the international field, the Community operates as an inter-governmental *bloc*, without requiring much sacrifice of sovereignty from the Member States—in short, precisely in the way that the pragmatists always said it should. Progress towards a more integrated Community, of the sort Monnet and Schuman dreamt of, has been slow or non-existent since the late 1960s; and the integration already achieved has been placed in jeopardy by the growing economic divergences of the middle 1970s and by the monetary instability to which they gave rise.

Yet, in spite of all this, the pragmatic view is both wrong and dangerous. It rests implicitly on the assumption that the Community can stay where it is: that the Member States can continue to enjoy the advantages of belonging to a strong intergovernmental *bloc*, without making new transfers of power to Community institutions. In fact, the one virtual certainty about the Community's future is that it cannot stay where it is. For it faces two great challenges, each of which is more formidable than is generally appreciated in the United Kingdom, and each of which will force it to choose between moving forward and moving back. If it is to move forward, power will have to be transferred from the national to the Community level on a scale without precedent in the Community's history. If it moves back, the survival of even the limited, 'negative' Community we know will be placed in jeopardy.

2

Forward or Back

The first great challenge now facing the Community is that of enlargement to the South. It is a complicated, even paradoxical, challenge, which can be understood only if it is placed in its historical context. As we have seen, the Community's most impressive achievements since the mid-1960s have been in the external field. Its internal development has hung fire; in some important respects, the *acquis communautaire* of the 1960s has been eroded in the 1970s. But as a trading and negotiating *bloc*, it has continued to grow in effectiveness and power. Because of its success as such, membership of it has become increasingly attractive to weaker countries on its periphery. Britain joined in 1973 because the British governing élite had come to believe that it would be unable to influence world affairs or to protect British interests if she remained outside. Now Greece, Portugal and Spain have applied for membership as well; though their motives differ in some important respects from Britain's, there can be no doubt that, for them, too, the Community's success in external affairs has been a major attraction. But external success may carry the seeds of its own destruction. The Community's external role is a function of its internal cohesion. It is a powerful negotiating *bloc* because it is a powerful trading *bloc*: and it is a powerful trading *bloc* because it is a common market, held together by an elaborate system of common rules, impartially enforced by a Court of Justice, whose writ runs throughout its territory. If there were no common market—and there would be no common market if there were no elaborate paraphernalia of regulations and directives— the cosy chats between foreign ministers and heads of government, to which the British attach so much importance, could not take place. Yet the larger the Community becomes, the bigger is the risk that its internal cohesion will be weakened, and that the foundations on which its external successes have been built will be undermined.

Britain provides the most obvious case in point. British entry in 1973 was unquestionably necessary for the Community. Another failure would have been enormously damaging to the credibility and authority of the Community's own institutions, and would have provoked an equally damaging bout of recrimination and bitterness among the Member States. But no one can deny that the present Community of Nine is less cohesive than was the old Community of Six. Vast quantities of scarce administrative time and talent have been needed to smooth over real or imagined differences of interest between Britain and the other members. More important still, the mere fact that nine Governments are represented in the Council of Ministers instead of six, and that as a result nine potential vetoes have to be taken into account instead of six, has made it even more difficult to reach decisions than it was before.

Now it looks as though history may repeat itself. Once again enlargement is a political imperative for the Community. The applicant countries are all unquestionably eligible for membership. A Europe that stopped at the Pyrenees or that excluded the cradle of European civilisation would be as unthinkable as a Europe that stopped at the Rhine or as a Europe that excluded Italy. Not only are the applicants all European, but they are all democracies. Not only are they all democracies, but they are the only countries in the world where democracy has won big victories in the last few years. For all of them, membership of the Community would be, among other things, a certificate of democratic respectability. To deny membership to them would imply — or would, at any rate, be taken by their peoples to imply — that they did not deserve such a certificate, that for some reason or another they were not worthy of full membership of the democratic West.

No one who remembers the effect which de Gaulle's first veto had on British attitudes to the Community can doubt that such an act of rejection would do great damage to their self-esteem, and that in such circumstances their commitments to democracy might be undermined as well. The Council of Ministers may have been wrong to override the Commission's cautious Opinion on the Greek application when it was put forward in 1976. But that is water under the bridge. Whatever may have been true in 1976, to slam the door on the applicants now would be to undermine democracy in the three countries where it has won its most resounding recent victories, and to endanger Western interests in areas of acute strategic importance. Yet if the door is left open, and no countervailing measures are taken, Community cohesion can hardly fail to suffer as it did after 1973.

It is true that there are important differences between Greece, Portugal and Spain on the one hand and Britain on the other. Britain joined for political, not economic, reasons. Once in, however, she presented a political problem to the rest of the Community much more than an economic one. To be sure, the British economy was much weaker than most Community economies; as everyone knows, the facts that Britain is a large food importer, and had been accustomed to protect farm incomes by imposing exchequer payments on the taxpayer rather than by imposing higher prices on the consumer, made it difficult for her to adjust to the common agricultural policy. But although her economic weaknesses created great problems for the British Government, they cannot really be said to have imposed big new burdens on the *Community*, while the problems caused by her special agricultural peculiarities might have been overcome if her Ministers had played their cards more skilfully. The reason some of the substantive economic problems associated with British membership have bulked large in Community discussions in the last few years is not that they in fact present great problems for the Community. It is that British ministers have wanted them to bulk large; and the reason British ministers have wanted them to bulk large is that there is a powerful anti-European faction in the Labour Party, to which many ministers belong and with which no ministers want to quarrel. This is not the place to examine the reasons for the strength and longevity of anti-Europeanism in the Labour Party: some of them have been discussed in the last chapter. What matters for our present purposes is that they are clearly political, not economic, in origin.

In the case of the latest applicants, the boot is likely to be on the other foot.[1] Supranationalism holds no terrors for them. Their Governments continually insist that they want to join a strong Community, and all the evidence suggests that they mean what they say. All see membership of the Community as a potential source of support in times of trouble; all appear to recognise that a cohesive Community would be able to offer more, and more reliable, support than a divided one. Apart from Denmark, the smaller, weaker members of the existing Community have followed a more *communautaire* line in Community affairs than the larger, stronger members have done. Greece and Portugal, whose populations are on a par with that of Belgium, will have as strong an interest in strengthening the supranational elements in the Community's constitution as the Benelux countries have had. Spain's population is significantly lower than that of the four big member states, and she will have no reason to be less *communautaire* than Italy. In all three applicant countries, moreover, membership of the Community has ideological as well as practical attractions. In all three, 'Europe' has meant democracy. It would be logical, therefore, if they were to conclude that the way to strengthen democracy is to strengthen Europe.

In economics, it is a different story. The economies of the three applicant countries are already so closely linked with the Community that their applications may have been inevitable on economic grounds alone once political circumstances made it feasible for them to apply. As we shall see, there are important differences between them. Spain is not only much bigger and more populous than Greece and Portugal. It is also much more advanced, with a larger and more competitive industrial sector, and a smaller agricultural one. All three, however, depend mainly on exports to the Community, on earnings from Community tourists and on remittances from emigrant workers in Community countries. None could end its dependence on the Community without sharp and painful changes in the whole orientation of its economy.[2] For all three, the choice lies, not between dependence and non-dependence on the Community, but between dependence on the Community together with a voice in its decisions from inside, and dependence with no voice outside. In spite of all this, however, enlargement will create severe social and economic problems for the Community, on a scale unequalled in its history. Since 1960, the economies of the applicant countries have all grown much faster than any existing Community economy has done. Even so, all three are still much poorer than the existing Community. The *per capita* income of Portugal, the poorest of the three, is only a third of the Community average. Spain's is 54 per cent of the Community's average, and that of Greece, 44 per cent. The corresponding figures for Ireland and Italy, the two poorest existing members, are 47 per cent and 59 per cent respectively.[3]

These figures do not tell the whole story, but they tell a large part of it. When Britain joined, an admittedly rather backward and inefficient mature industrial society had to be assimilated by a Community of mature industrial societies. The present applicants are not mature industrial societies at all. Though Spain's development has gone much further than that of Greece and Portugal, they are all developing countries. Their economic and social structures differ in a whole series of ways from those of Northern Europe, and they cannot be assimilated into a 'northern' Community, based on 'northern' assumptions, without a number of painful changes.

The most obvious difference is that they all depend much more heavily on agriculture than does the existing Community. It is true that the share of their Gross Domestic Products accounted for by agriculture has declined rapidly—in Spain's case dramatically—over the last fifteen years. In 1961, agriculture accounted for more than a quarter of Spain's gross domestic product. Today, it accounts for only a tenth. In Greece, the figure fell over the same period from a little more than a quarter to less than a fifth and in Portugal from a quarter to one-eighth. The percentage of the labour force engaged in agriculture has fallen too—from two-fifths to one-fifth in Spain, from a half to a third in Greece and from two-fifths to a third in Portugal. But although these figures are much lower than they were, they are still much higher than the comparable figure of 9 per cent in the existing Community. Agricultural productivity in the applicant countries, moreover, is less than half that of the existing Community. On present-day figures, enlargement would increase the size of the Community's agricultural labour force by 55 per cent, but its total output by only 24 per cent. The applicants' farmers are not only less productive than those of the existing Community; many of them operate on a much smaller scale. In Greece, the average size of a farm is 4 hectares, compared with 7.7 hectares in Italy and 57 hectares in the United Kingdom. The Portuguese and Spanish averages are higher — 10 hectares in Portugal and 23 in Spain — but in Portugal and Spain, farms vary so much in size that averages are almost meaningless. Less than a tenth of Portuguese farms are bigger than 20 hectares, and less than a fifth of Spanish farms. In all three countries, in short, the vast majority of farms are still small, poor and inefficient.

In spite of the importance of agriculture in their economies, moreover, Spain and Portugal are net importers of food, while only Greece is a net exporter. In Spain and Portugal, the balance of trade in agricultural products has deteriorated dramatically in recent years. In the early 1960s, 94 per cent of Spain's agricultural imports were covered by agricultural exports. Ten years later the figure was 73 per cent. In Portugal, the 'cover rate' declined, over the same ten-year period, from 100 per cent to 45 per cent. To make matters worse, a large proportion of the applicants' agricultural exports is in 'sensitive' products, which are in surplus in the existing Community. Fresh and processed fruit and vegetables account for more than half of Spain's agricultural exports and for nearly 60 per cent of those of Greece. Wine accounts for an eighth of Spain's agricultural exports and for 40 per cent of Portugal's.

The industrial picture is more complicated, but not, for that reason, more comforting. All the applicant countries have achieved rapid industrial growth. In all of them industrial growth deserves the lion's share of the credit for increased living standards; in all of them industry accounts for a large proportion of the Gross Domestic Product, and employs a significant proportion of the working population. But the applicants' growth has been lop-sided within the industrial sector as well as between industry and agriculture. As in many industrialising countries, their Governments have followed highly mercantilist policies—protecting their old industries with a variety of tariff and non-tariff barriers, and attracting foreign investment with a variety of incentives, often linked directly to export performance. The result is a badly unbalanced industrial structure. In each, there is a highly competitive, efficient, export-orientated, 'advanced' sector, to a considerable extent foreign-owned, and well-suited to take advantage of the opportunities which entry into the Community will bring. In each, there is also an inefficient, uncompetitive, 'backward' sector, with a multiplicity of small firms which stand to lose far more from Community competition than they can conceivably gain from access to Community markets. In Portugal, 84 per cent of the total number of enterprises employ fewer than 50 people; only 0.3 per cent employ more than 1,000. Three-quarters of the smallest firms, with fewer than 10 employees apiece, are concentrated in the traditional sectors of foodstuffs, textiles, clothing, footwear and cork—all of them, products which are now in difficulties. In Spain 72 per cent of the total number of firms employ fewer than 5 workers, and only 0.2 per cent employ more than 500. In Greece—where 60 per cent of the total labour force is self-employed—94 per cent of firms employ fewer than 10 workers and only 1.8 per cent more than 30.

The lop-sidedness of the applicants' growth over the last fifteen years is also reflected in gross regional imbalances. The *per capita* income of the Greater Athens region is more than one-and-a-half times the Greek national average. That of Epirus, the poorest region, is 61 per cent of the national average. The *per capita* income of the Lisbon region is almost three times that of the poorest Portuguese region, and well above the national average, while the *per capita* income of every other region is below it. In Spain, regional imbalances are not as marked, but even in Spain the four richest provinces have *per capita* incomes ranging from 132 per cent to 140 per cent of the national average, while the *per capita* incomes of the four poorest range from 76 per cent of the national average to 93 per cent. As one would expect, industry—and, still more, 'advanced' industry, of course—is concentrated in a small area. In five out of the seven Portuguese regions, between 44 per cent and 69 per cent of the working population is employed in agriculture;

in nine of the ten Greek regions the figure ranges from 45 per cent to 73 per cent. Even in Spain, more than 20 per cent of the labour force is employed in agriculture in 41 provinces out out of 50, more than 30 per cent in 31 provinces, and more than 40 per cent in 17 provinces.

Enlargement and the Community Institutions

In the absence of strong countervailing policies, entry into the Community would almost certainly make many of these problems worse. In the first place, it can be expected to damage the applicant countries' balances of payments, at any rate in the short run. Spain and Portugal, as net food importers, will suffer in balance-of-payments terms from the application of the common agricultural policy. All three are likely to lose more, initially at least, from dropping their own tariff and non-tariff barriers against imports from the Community than they will gain from the disappearance of the Community's tariffs against imports from them. More ominously, entry is likely to worsen their regional and social imbalances. Almost by definition, the 'advanced' sectors of their industries, which will benefit from tariff-free entry into Community markets, are concentrated in their most prosperous regions; their poorer regions depend much more heavily on the 'backward' sectors which will find it hard to withstand Community competition. Agricultural competition, too, will have perverse regional consequences. The applicant countries can compete successfully in 'Mediterranean' foodstuffs, but they are uncompetitive in cereals, livestock and dairy produce; and the latter are produced mainly in their less prosperous regions. On balance, Spain is likely to do well out of membership — too well, perhaps to suit some existing member states — but even Spain will have to face some difficult problems of adjustment. Membership is necessary for Portugal and Greece as well, but unless its effects are mitigated, the regional and social price is likely to be very high.

The existing Community will have to pay a price for enlargement too. Just as the weaker applicant regions are likely to suffer most from Community competition, so the weaker Community regions will suffer most from the applicants' competition. The applicant countries are competitive in Mediterranean food-stuffs and in such industrial products as textiles, clothing, footwear, ships and steel—all sectors which are in difficulties in the existing Community and which are found disproportion-ately in the weaker regions of the existing Community. At the same time, the regional imbalances of the enlarged Community will be far more severe than those of the existing Community. The total population of the Community will increase by 53 million. Thirty-four million of the newcomers will be living in regions with a *per capita* income on a par with that of the Italian Mezzogiorno or the West of Ireland. To put the same point another way round, the *per capita* income of Hamburg, the Community's richest region, is six times as large as the West of Ireland's. It is twelve times as large as that of the poorest Portuguese region.

All this will place heavy new burdens on institutions which can hardly cope with the burdens they already have to bear. Battles over resource allocation are bitter enough in the existing Community, as bleary-eyed Ministers emerging from a dawn Agriculture Council would be the first to testify. They are likely to be much more bitter in the enlarged Community. It is true that the direct cost of enlargement to the Community budget will be smaller than is sometimes realised. A recent Commission study shows that if the applicants had all become full members of the Community in 1978, and if all the Community's existing policies had been applied to them, the net cost to the budget would have been 1,000 million units of account, or about one-thirteenth of the present Budget. But that only proves that the Community's existing policies are incapable of meeting the objective set out in the Rome Treaty, by which the signatories committed themselves to ensure the 'harmonious development' of their economies and to reduce 'the differences existing between the various regions'. The fact is that the present Budget is hopelessly unprogressive, and that the economic and social problems which enlargement will bring with it will be solved only with different policies and a far more redistributive Budget. The precise budgetary cost of enlargement on the assumption of unchanged policies therefore provides no guide whatever to the likely political consequences of enlargement.

What matters is that it will bring more new claims on resources than new resources: that the amount of jam available for spreading will increase by only a small amount, while the amount of bread on which the jam has to be spread will increase by a very large amount. More farmers—and far more poorer farmers—will be growing crops which are already in surplus. There will be sharper conflicts of interest between 'southern' and 'northern' agriculture, and between both and the consumer. More unemployed workers will be looking for jobs and more uncompetitive industries will be looking for assistance. More interests will be clamouring for more exceptions to the system of common rules on which the Community is based; more politically sensitive corns will have to be avoided by those who operate it. New difficulties will appear even in fields of activity unconnected with resource allocation. There is an obvious conflict of interest between the applicant countries and a number of non-Community Mediterranean countries with which the Community has made agreements. At a time of high unemployment, there is also an uglier conflict of interest between the applicants and the richer member countries over the interpretation of the provisions of the Rome Treaty guaranteeing the free movement of labour. At yet a different, but still important level, more languages will be spoken in the Council of Ministers and the European Parliament, more documents will be held up by translation difficulties and more national administrations will be fighting for a fair share of senior posts in the Commission. Above all, more Governments will be taking part in an already creaking decision-making process, in which all Governments have to agree to—or at least to acquiesce in—all the decisions that matter.

Enlargement would create institutional problems for the Community even if the applicants were rich, 'northern' countries. It is, however, the fact that they are poor, 'southern' countries which creates the social and economic problems, and it is because the social and economic problems exist that the institutional problems matter as much as they do. But the social and economic gap between 'southern' applicants and a largely 'northern' Community cannot be closed by pious assertions of Community solidarity on the part of the old members, or even by heroic acts of will on the part of the new ones. The applicant countries cannot pull themselves up by their own bootstraps. Theirs are coat-tail economies, whose fortunes vary with the fortunes of the stronger economies on which they depend. Fifty per cent of their trade is with the Community; they can expand their economies only if the Community's economies expand. A return to high rates of growth in the Community would make it possible for them to return to their own even higher rates of a few years ago, and thus to narrow the development gap between themselves and northern Europe. So long as the Community stagnates, they will remain locked in by a vicious circle of low productivity and high unemployment. If they are to achieve living standards comparable with those of northern Europe they will have to raise their productivity to north-European levels, and they can raise their levels of productivity only by moving labour out of agriculture and the backward sectors of their industries. But they cannot move labour out of low-productivity sectors if there is nowhere for it to go; and expansion in the high-productivity sectors depends on a resumption of growth beyond their frontiers.

The Economic Malaise

At this point the challenge of enlargement is linked with the second big challenge now facing the Community—that of the economic malaise in which it has been engulfed for more than five years. The inflationary fever that followed the 1973 energy crisis is now subsiding, but only at the cost of sluggish growth and rising unemployment. At the end of 1977, the year-on-year inflation rate for the Community as a whole was around 9 per cent, compared with more than 11 per cent at the end of 1976; according to Commission estimates it was less than 7 per cent at the end of 1978. More encouraging still, the improvement has been particularly marked in the most inflation-prone countries. But in 1977 output grew by only a little more than 2 per cent, while the unemployment rate went up from 5 per cent to 5.5 per cent. In 1978, it is true, output began to recover but unemployment remained obstinately high. According to Commission estimates, community G.D.P. grew in volume by 2.6 per cent, as against 2.3 per cent the year before. But the unemployment rate rose slightly from 5.5 per cent to 5.7 per cent. The surplus economies, moreover, performed no better than the deficit ones. Output in Federal Germany grew by 2.8 per cent in 1977 and by 2.7 per cent in 1978, while the corresponding figures for France were 3 per cent and 3 per cent.[4]

In the Community as a whole, six million people were out of work in 1978 — forty per cent of them aged less than 25.[5] At the same time, the old engines of economic growth appear to have run out of steam. One of the main causes of the boom of the late 1960s was the rapid growth in intra-Community trade. In 1977, intra-Community trade grew by only 2 per cent, as against an annual average of 9 per cent in the previous decade. Meanwhile, demographic forces beyond anyone's control are making the problem more acute. In the next seven years, according to Commission estimates, nine million more young people will enter the Community's labour market than old people will leave it.[6] It is true that, at the end of 1978, the Commission saw a chink of light appearing; and in its annual report for 1978–79 it forecast 'gradual rather than dramatic economic recovery'. Its figures were, however, less optimistic than its words. Though output was expected to grow by 3.5 per cent in 1979, as against 2.6 per cent in 1978, the unemployment rate was expected to stick at 5.6 per cent.[7]

The Threat of Protectionism

Continued unemployment poses an equally severe — if a less immediately apparent — threat to the Community's cohesion. So far, it is true, the unity of the market has not been seriously undermined. In its relations with the outside world, the Community has lurched towards a slightly shamefaced protectionism, notably in steel, shipbuilding and textiles, but in their relations with each other the Member States have made only covert breaches in the free-trade principles on which the Community is based. In Britain, the minority Callaghan

Government has staunchly resisted left-wing calls for an 'alternative strategy', designed to insulate the British economy from the international economic system of which it is a part. In France, the Union of the Left, whose economic and social policies could have been carried out in practice only in a siege economy, was roundly defeated at the polls. In Germany, the governing Social Democrats and opposition Christian Democrats vie with each other in professions of free-trade faith.

Yet this state of affairs is more precarious than it looks. The Community can put forward strong social and humanitarian arguments for keeping out imports from more efficient producers in the sectors mentioned above. It is true that its steel, ship-building and textile industries need restructuring and that it will take time to restructure them. It is true that if they are exposed to outside competition before they have been restructured, many steel, shipyard and textile workers will lose their jobs, and that the already menacing unemployment figures will be swollen still further. Unfortunately, however, precisely the same arguments can be put forward for a resort to protectionism on the part of one Member State of the Community against other Member States. If it is right to protect German shipyard workers against Japanese competition, why should it be wrong to protect British car workers from German competition? If it is legitimate to keep cheap Korean textiles out of the Community, why is it illegitimate to keep cheap Italian textiles out of the United Kingdom? Questions like these are likely to be heard more and more frequently if unemployment remains at its present level. The answer that Germany and Italy are fellow-members of the Community, whereas Japan and Korea are not, is likely to seem more compelling to officials in the Commission's Directorate-General for the Internal Market and Industrial Affairs than to car workers in Coventry or to hosiery workers in Mansfield.

Covert restrictions on intra-Community trade are already more frequent than is generally appreciated. In the summer of 1978, Commissioner Davignon warned his colleagues that there had been a 'proliferation' of such restrictions of late, and explained that although the Commission was already examining more than 400 cases of alleged interference with the free movement of goods, that figure gave only a 'partial idea' of the true dimensions of the problem.[8] This situation, moreover, developed before the depth and gravity of the present crisis were fully appreciated. Official forecasts, after all, suggested that growth in 1977 would be twice what it actually was. If business-men and trade unionists had known how black the truth was going to be, protectionist pressures in the Member States would almost certainly have been much stronger than they were. Already, there are signs that these pressures are mounting: the trade unions' patience, to take one crucial example, is clearly wearing thin.[9] And, in the present climate, it would only need one Government to make a really big breach in the free-trade front for a kind of domino theory of trade restriction to apply throughout the Community. The Community countries are not likely ever again to engage in old-fashioned tariff wars against each other. But protectionism has many faces, and tariffs are only one of them. The range of instruments with which a modern Government can protect home producers against foreign competition is enormously wide, ranging from nationally-biased quality and packaging controls at one end of the spectrum to outright quantitative restrictions at the other end. Widespread resort to any of them would destroy the unity of the market and the procedures by which it is maintained; as we have seen, these are the foundations on which the whole Community structure is based. Abraham Lincoln once said that the United States could not survive 'half-free' and 'half-slave'. The Community would find it equally difficult to survive—in politics as well as in economics—with half its members committed to trade liberalisation and half of them engaged in a surreptitious retreat into autarchy.

Majority Voting

It will not be easy to overcome these challenges. There is no hope of doing so unless significantly more power is transferred from the national to the Community level. This is most obviously true of the challenge of enlargement. As we have seen, the applicant countries insist that they want to join a strong Community, not a diluted one. Moreover, their interests would be served better by membership of a strong one. Yet their wishes, and even their interests, are in a sense immaterial. Few car buyers wish to be held up in traffic jams and none has an interest in being held up, but if too many new cars appear on unsuitable old roads, traffic jams occur just the same. Anyone who has ever served on any kind of committee can see that it is bound to be more difficult to get twelve countries, at markedly different stages of development and therefore with highly divergent interests, to reach agreement than it is to get nine countries, whose interests and circumstances do not diverge so much, to do so. If agreements are not to take even longer to reach than they do now, those taking part in the arguments which precede agreement will have to be more prepared to give way than they are now. This means, in practice, that the existing Member States, as well as the newcomers, will have to be more willing to subordinate what they see as their own interests to a majority view of the Community interest. And that, in turn, means that the institutional balance will have to be changed, so as to give more weight to the interests of the Community as a whole and less to the separate interests of the Member States.

There is room for argument about the best way to do this. But one point is clear. As we have seen, the 1966 Luxembourg Compromise had three consequences, each pernicious. By making it possible for each Member State to insist on unanimity whenever it wanted to, it ensured that Community decision-making would be extraordinarily slow-moving, and at the same time extraordinarily jerky. More important, it also ensured that decisions would be taken in the wrong way and according to the wrong criteria. In any union, there is bound to be a tension between the interest of the whole and the interests of the parts, between centripetal forces making for more cohesion and centrifugal ones making for less. No one who has studied the history of the Community over the last fifteen years can dispute that the centrifugal forces have become stronger than they were and the centripetal ones weaker, or that—on the assumption that it was worth while setting up a Community at all—the interests of the whole receive less attention than they ought to do in comparison with the interests of the parts.

In policy area after policy area — aerospace, labour-market policy, industrial restructuring, energy — the Community's citizens would be better served by strong Community policies, applied through the Community's territory, than by a mish-mash of national policies. Yet in all these areas, strong Community policies are conspicuous by their absence. Though it would be absurd to suggest that the Community's failure to develop policies in these areas is solely due to its institutional structure, its institutional structure undoubtedly bears a large part of the blame. For that structure makes it extraordinarily difficult for the Community interest to prevail. And among the reasons why it does so are the effects of the Luxembourg Compromise on the way in which the Council of Ministers goes about its business and on the relationship between the Council and the Commission. For as well as making it more difficult to take decisions quickly, the Luxembourg Compromise ensured that the Council of Ministers would be less a Community institution, seeking to further its view of the Community interest, than a forum for inter-state bargaining, the eventual outcome of which is a compromise between Member Governments' views of their separate national interests. Finally, it ensured that the Commission — which, for all its faults, does at least have a Community mandate and, at any rate in theory, the capacity to form a coherent view of the interests of the Community as a whole — would lose power to the Member Governments, whose viewpoints can never be more than national.

In recent years, it is true, more decisions have been taken by majority vote than was the case in the heyday of Gaullism. But so long as Member Governments retain the power to impose a veto in areas where majority voting should apply under the Treaty it makes comparatively little difference to the balance of Community power whether decisions are in fact taken by a majority or not. Despite recent moves towards majority voting in practice, the Luxembourg Compromise is still a kind of Banquo's Ghost at every Community feast, paralysing the guests into immobility by the mere fact of its gibbering presence at the head of the table. So long as it is in force, the Council will continue to move at the pace of the slowest, and the Commission will continue to be inhibited from playing the active, initiatory role assigned to it by the Treaties.

After enlargement, however, rapid movement and bold initiatives will be essential. It is an illusion to think that the development gap between the newcomers and the existing Community can be closed by some dramatic act of generosity on the morrow (or even on the eve) of accession, or alternatively by long-drawn-out transitional arrangements designed to temper the wind of Community rules to the shorn lamb of the newcomers' backwardness. Dramatic acts of generosity are going to be needed, and so are lengthy transitional arrangements, but the gap — and its associated conflicts of interest — will still be there after any conceivable transitional period has come to an end. These conflicts need not be fatal to the Community, any more than conflicts of interest between Lancashire and London are fatal to the United Kingdom. The newcomers and existing members have common interests as well; and the interests which they have in common are, in fact, stronger than the interests which divide them. If the institutional structure were overhauled so as to give due weight to these common interests, the Community would be more cohesive after enlargement than before. But the 'if' is a big one. If no changes are made, if a decision-making machine which is manifestly unable to handle the Community's existing conflicts of interest satisfactorily is asked to handle new conflicts as well, the result will be more indecision, more delay and more frequent deadlock. If that result is to be avoided, Member Governments will have to be prepared, not just to take more decisions by a majority than they do now, but to commit themselves clearly and unequivocally to the principle of majority voting, as a minimum in the areas where it was envisaged in the Treaty and if possible in other areas as well.[10] There is no question but that such a commitment would entail a big transfer of power from national to Community level.

Monetary Union

The economic crisis points — less obviously, perhaps, but at least as urgently — in the same direction. It is not because they are indifferent or incompetent that the Governments of the

Community have failed to end the recession. It is because the classical nation state, having dominated the European political stage for the last 300 years, and having acquired immense new economic powers as a result of the Keynesian Revolution thirty or forty years ago, has been made obsolete by the growing economic interdependence of the recent past. Keynes's great achievement was to make the nation state master in its own economic house for the first time: to enable national Governments to determine the level of economic activity for themselves, independently of the world-wide trend. Since his death, however, the environment within which Governments have to operate has been transformed, at any rate in Europe. The member countries of the European Community live by taking in each others' washing. They all depend much more heavily on foreign trade than they used to do, and 50 per cent of their foreign trade is with each other. The economy has, so to speak, burst the bounds of the polity. In these circumstances, a national Government seeking to force economic activity up to a higher level than that of the rest of Europe is like an inexperienced swimmer caught by a sudden tide. It can swim rapidly back to the safety of the shore, or it can drown. What it cannot do is to plough gallantly on until it reaches its destination.

Hence the collapse of the so-called 'locomotive' theory, which held that if the Germans could be bullied into reflating more than they wanted to, the rest of the Community would be pulled along behind them. The Germans refused to oblige — partly, no doubt, because the chief proponent of the theory, namely the British Chancellor of the Exchequer, had few obvious qualifications for teaching other people how to run their economies. But that was not the chief reason for their reluctance. Much more important was that they knew that their levels of investment and employment depend as much on the levels of demand in the countries which buy German goods as on the level of demand in Germany itself; and that they feared, with some reason, that if they tried to reflate unilaterally, the result would be more inflation, not more output or more jobs. Hence also the strange spectacle of Messrs Callaghan, Foot and Healey applying deflationary monetary and incomes policies with a zeal worthy of Philip Snowden. For if unilateral reflation is ruled out for the strong, it is even more obviously ruled out for the weak. Unilateral reflation in a weak economy would lead, by way of a deteriorating balance of payments and a depreciating currency, to higher inflation and yet more currency depreciation. It would not lead to faster growth or lower unemployment—or not for long. In the early stages of the recession, after all, the British and Italians both tried to prop up employment with deficit financing on traditional Keynesian lines. Both failed, with disastrous results.

This does not mean, however, that the traditional Keynesian instruments can no longer be used at all. It means that, in a continent as interdependent economically as Europe has become, they can be used successfully only at a continental level. The Member States of the Community therefore have three options. The first is to sit back and do nothing, in the hope that the economy will recover of its own accord. The second is to break with interdependence and retreat—no doubt slowly and without open acknowledgment—into a present-day version of the autarchy of the 1930s. The third is to accept the logic of interdependence, and find a way of applying Keynes's teaching on a continental, rather than on a merely national, scale. For the reasons already given, the first option is politically unrealistic as well as irrational and inhumane. The real choice lies between the second and third. The second, autarchic option would tear the Community apart. If the Community is to survive, only the third is left.

This was the logic underlying the decision which the Commission took in 1977 to re-launch its old campaign for monetary union. Much the same logic underlay Chancellor Schmidt's campaign to persuade his Community partners to establish a European Monetary System. Monetary union would not bring about recovery all by itself. By ending the exchange-rate uncertainties which at present inhibit recovery in the strong and weak economies alike, it would, however, create a framework within which recovery could be pursued with some hope of success. But the logic leads to a harsher and politically less palatable conclusion as well. Monetary union is like marriage, not like chastity. You can be more or less chaste, but you cannot be more or less married. Nor can you have more or less monetary union: either you have it or you do not. Even in the truncated form finally agreed upon in December 1978, the European monetary system will be of considerable value as a staging post to complete monetary union. But it will be of value only if it is a staging post. If it is a substitute, and seen as a substitute, it will do more harm than good.

The point of the exercise is to eliminate exchange-rate uncertainty; and after the experience of the last ten years no one is going to believe that exchange-rate changes have been ruled out in anything short of a monetary union. Exchange rates change because inflation-rates differ; so long as the member countries of the Community have different rates of inflation they will be under pressure to change their exchange rates accordingly. The lesson of the last ten years is that such pressures are, in the end, irresistible, and that attempts to resist them are as costly as they are futile. King Canute got his feet wet trying to convince his courtiers that he could not hold back the tide. Monetary Canutes are apt to suffer in more expensive ways. The currency markets know this and behave accordingly: and, in free economies, the market rules. Britain and France left the Snake, after all, because they were forced to, not because they wanted to; and they were forced to because the currency markets knew that their inflation-rates differed so much from Germany's that they would sooner or later have to change the value of their currencies in relation to Germany's. The E.M.S. will make no difference to inflation rates; and if the currency markets see it as nothing more than a new version of the Snake they will sooner or later destroy it as they destroyed the Snake. Complete monetary union is, however, a different matter. In a monetary union, exchange-rate changes between the members are, by definition, impossible. Monetary union, in short, is the only adequate solution to the problem. The E.M.S. will work only if the currency markets are convinced that it is intended to lead to monetary union, and that the destination will be reached before very long. They can be convinced only if it is accompanied by other measures to overcome the obstacles to monetary union; and as the British, Italians and Irish have all realised (though without drawing the same practical conclusion for their own national policies) the chief obstacle is that the weaker economies could not sustain membership of a monetary union without substantial resource transfer from the strong.

It follows that monetary union is impossible without a big increase in the size and redistributive power of the Community Budget. As we have seen, the Community Budget accounts at present for less than 1.0 per cent of the total Community G.D.P., and it does virtually nothing to reduce income differences between the Member States. The MacDougall Group of economists have shown that in fully-fledged federal states like West Germany, Australia and the United States, the federal budget accounts for around 20 per cent of G.D.P.; and that the net effect of the federal budget is, among other things, to reduce state income differentials by around 35 per cent.[11] They have also shown, however, that—provided it were deliberately tailored with this aim in view—it would be possible to construct a Community Budget capable of reducing income differentials by around 40 per cent and accounting for only between 5 and 7 per cent of Community G.D.P., and that it would be possible for a Budget which accounted for only around 2.5 per cent of G.D.P. to reduce income differentials by about 10 per cent.

Their finding has revolutionary political implications. It is clear that monetary union would impose insupportable burdens on the weaker members unless resources were deliberately redistributed in their favour. What the MacDougall Group have shown, however, is that it is possible to achieve as much redistribution as is achieved in fully federal states with a very much smaller budget. If monetary union required a Community Budget that accounted for as large a proportion of G.D.P. as the federal budget of West Germany or the United States, it would obviously be politically impractical, at any rate until a remote and unforeseeable future. But a Community Budget accounting for 5 to 7 per cent of G.D.P. is a practical proposition, provided that Member States have the will to achieve it. The same applies, *a fortiori*, to the smaller Budget accounting for around 2.5 per cent of total Community G.D.P. which the MacDougall Group consider appropriate for what they term 'pre-federal integration'.

The second political point to emerge from the MacDougall

Report is, however, that although these figures are very small in comparison with the equivalent figures in fully-federal states, they are very large in relation to the existing Community. Full-scale monetary union would require a Community Budget six or seven times bigger than the present one, and it would also require a deliberately redistributive Budget, carefully designed to take resources away from the richer Member States and give them to the poorer. Such a Budget would clearly be in the interests of the richer Member States. Almost by definition, they have most to lose from the break-up of the Common Market and a lurch back into protectionism; and, as we have seen, monetary union provides the only sure way of keeping the Common Market together. Behind the MacDougall Group's statistical tables and guarded prose lie, in fact, the outlines of a mutually beneficial deal between the rich and poor Member States of the Community which, in a rational world at any rate, would be acceptable politically to both. The poor would benefit from resource transfers. The rich would benefit from the survival of the structure which has made them rich. But such a deal would, of course, involve a major transfer of power to the Community and away from the Member States.

So, for that matter, would the non-budgetary aspects of monetary union. Two of the most highly-prized weapons in the armoury of the modern, post-Keynesian state are control over the money supply and control over the exchange rate. If monetary union is to come into being in the Community, both will have to be placed in a Community armoury instead.

Thus, the choice is stark: either much more majority voting in the Council of Ministers, with all that implies for the balance of power between national and Community authorities, or the virtual seizing-up of the Community's decision-making machinery; either the transfer of two critically important instruments of economic policy from national to Community hands, and a 700 per cent increase in the size of the Community budget, or continued unemployment and the slow erosion of the foundations on which the Community is built. One way or another the choice will have to be made. It would be better to make it by design than by default.

3

The Institutional
Imbalance

The challenges described in the last chapter can be overcome
only if more power is transferred from the national to the
Community level. But suggestions that power should be transferred from the national to the Community level have been made
more than once in the last ten years, and little power has in
fact been transferred. If more progress is to be made in the
next ten years than in the last, it is not enough to assert that
progress is desirable. It is also necessary to enquire—and in a
much more tough-minded fashion than is common in Community circles—into the reasons why it has not been made.

A favourite explanation among Commission officials is that
it is all the fault of the 1973 energy crisis. Before 1973, the
the argument goes, the Community was on the verge of rapid
progress. It had, no doubt, stagnated in the middle and late
1960s. But when de Gaulle left the stage in 1969 the situation
improved. The 1969 Hague Summit put forward an ambitious
programme for the 1970s. The Werner Plan for monetary
union was put forward. The thorny problems of British membership, which had lingered uneasily on the agenda of Community
politics since the early 1950s, was settled at last. The 1972 Paris
Summit agreed on new goals for the 1970s, and in the course
of 1973 considerable progress was made towards them. Britain,
Ireland and Denmark were assimilated into the Community
structure. A Commissioner for regional policy took up office in
Brussels and a Community regional policy was hammered out.
But for the Yom Kippur War, the increase in oil prices which

followed, and the economic dislocation they caused, progress would have continued.

The reason it did not occur was simply that the Community had not developed far enough before the crisis broke. Inevitably the strong economies suffered less than the weak; as a result the existing divergences in inflation rates, and, indeed, in other indices of economic performance, became even more marked. Given increasing divergence between the strong and weak economies, the abandonment of the Werner Plan and the collapse of the 'snake' were equally inevitable. However, this argument continues, the worst effects of the crisis are now behind us. Slowly, with great difficulty, but nevertheless unmistakeably, the Member States of the Community are forcing their inflation rates down to tolerable levels. Though they have not yet brought unemployment down as well, they have turned the really awkward corner; as a result, the Community is moving forward once again. Important new initiatives have been made by the Commission. The decision to hold direct elections to the European Parliament is being implemented. The enlargement negotiations are under way. The Commission has effectively won the right to be represented at so-called 'economic summits'. The elements of a Community industrial policy are now being assembled. There is, therefore, no need for despondency. The Community has had three setbacks in its history. The first came when de Gaulle vetoed British membership in 1963. The second came with the crisis that ended in the 1966 Luxembourg Compromise. The third followed the oil crisis. On each occasion, despite defeatism and pessimism, the Community emerged satisfactorily in the end. The history of the last six years, as of the last sixteen, is a testimony to its vitality and resilience, not to its weakness.

At first sight, this argument looks quite plausible. It is true that the Community has suffered serious setbacks in the past, and that it has always recovered. It is true that the oil crisis did great damage to it. It is true that the divergences in inflation rates and exchange rates which were let loose by that crisis, and which came near to wrecking the Community between 1973 and 1976, are now abating. Finally, it is true that the Member States (though with the notable exception of the United Kingdom) have recently been prepared to make and accept *communautaire* initiatives of a much more radical kind than was the case during the last Commission's term of office. But it does not follow that the Community's recent troubles were solely due to the oil crisis, or that all is well now that the crisis is over. Crisis is double-edged. Sometimes, a crisis generates a mood of narrow and short-sighted *sauve qui peut*. At other times, crises shake their victims out of old attitudes and old assumptions, and make them more willing to collaborate than they were before. The Community is, after all, the child of crisis. It was the political and diplomatic crises of the late 1940s — the beginning of the Cold War, the Soviet occupation of Czechoslovakia, the Berlin air lift and the Korean War — that led the original member states of the Coal and Steel Community to put aside ancient hatreds and work together. There is no inherent reason why the oil crisis could not have had the same effect. It is, in short, bad logic and bad history to lay all the blame for the Community's failure to move forward in the 1970s on the oil crisis. What needs to be explained is the Member Governments' reaction to that crisis. To do that, it is necessary to dig deeper.

Nationalism and Supranationalism

Another explanation — much favoured by the present occupants of the two front benches in the British House of Commons — is that it would have been Utopian to expect anything else: that the Community has failed to move forward in the last few years because it has gone as far as it is capable of going: and that it has gone as far as it can because the peoples of the Community will never develop supranational loyalties remotely comparable in force and depth to the loyalties which they feel towards their own countries. The social, cultural and economic differences between the peoples of the Community go too deep to be eradicated by a politician's decree. So long as they remain, Monnet's vision of a supranational Europe transcending the nation state will remain a vision.

This argument needs careful examination. If it were valid,

there would indeed be no point in trying to create a more supra-national Europe. Clearly, there is much to be said for it. It is true that the nation state is still the focus for non-hedonistic loyalties of the sort which need to be called patriotic. It is true that such attempts as have been made from time to time to develop a higher, 'European' loyalty among ordinary citizens —by appropriating Beethoven's 9th Symphony as a European anthem, for example, or by urging yachtsmen to 'sail for Europe' —have been unsuccessful, and at the same time faintly embarrassing. It is true that there are social, cultural and economic differences between the peoples of the Community, and that no one in his senses imagines that these can (or should) be eradicated quickly or easily.

But the argument should not be allowed to rest there. In the first place, the kind of supranationalism which is now required in the Community would not impinge much on the concerns of the ordinary citizen. Monetary union would entail trans-ferring control over the exchange rate and the money supply from national to Community authorities. But the pros and cons of exchange-rate and monetary policy are not matters of hot debate in workingmen's clubs in the North of England or among *boules* players in Provence. The level and composition of taxation and public expenditure—which do impinge directly on the ordinary citizen—would still be matters for national Governments and national Parliaments. A prior commitment to engage in more majority voting in the Council of Ministers would undoubtedly entail a significant loss of power by Member Governments and, at any rate in theory, by national Parlia-ments. It is doubtful if the ordinary citizen would notice. The best guide to what will be needed in the next stage of integration is that contained in the MacDougall Report; and, as we have seen, the authors estimated that it would be possible to sustain a monetary union with a Community budget far smaller in proportion to G.D.P. than that of any modern unitary State, or even than that of any modern federation. Social and welfare services—which account for more than half of public expendi-ture in the Community's Member States—would be left in national hands. And it is, of course, overwhelmingly in that field that the ordinary citizen comes face to face with the public authorities. The Community's national differences may perhaps go too deep to permit the creation of a federal structure modelled on that of the United States, though even that is by no means self-evident, but federalism *à l'Americaine* is not what is needed. What is needed is the transfer of certain vitally important, but limited, powers from national Governments, which can no longer use them effectively, to Community authorities which could. That transfer could perfectly well be accompanied by much bigger downward transfers of power from national Governments to regional or provincial authorities. If it were, the distribution of power in the Community would be more decentralised than it is today, not less. This combination of more centralisation in fields where it is needed, and more decentralisation in fields where it is possible, might well be unpopular with self-important national politicians and power-hungry national civil servants. It would accord much more closely with the cultural, social and economic realities of modern Europe than does the present distribution.[1]

For although it is true that the nation state, rather than some nebulous 'Europe', remains the focus for non-hedonistic loyalties on the part of its citizens, it is also true that the nation state now faces powerful rivals for such loyalties. The United Kingdom provides the best example. Few British citizens feel much loyalty to the European Community. Far more feel loyal to the British nation state. Yet more and more British citizens in the non-English parts of the United Kingdom are beginning to feel quite strong loyalties to as yet unclassified entities, which may or may not become nation states at some time in the future but are certainly not nation states at the moment, and which have nevertheless acquired an emotional reality for those concerned. In France, despite a tradition of ferocious centralism going back to the seventeenth century if not before, the Bretons, the Basques, the Catalans, the Alsatians and the Provençals are all beginning to assert a non-French identity, and are increasingly reluctant to accept that the classical French nation state should be the only focus for their emotional loyalties. The Belgian nation state has almost been torn apart by the conflict between French-speakers and Flemish-speakers, and no longer commands much loyalty from anyone. Germany is already a federal republic, not a nation state of the classical kind; and there are strong, non-national loyalties in many of the German Länder. In the Italian South and in Sicily and Sardinia localist feelings are equally strong. The fact is that the notion of the nation state as the *sole* focus for non-hedonistic loyalty no longer stands up.

This has a number of implications for the pragmatic British view that cultural and social differences between the peoples of the Community make it impossible to move in a supranational direction. If—as seems likely—the emergence of the buried nations of Western Europe were to result in increasing political decentralisation on the lines of what has happened in Belgium, and of what is now happening in Great Britain, is it not at least possible that the new authorities which would have to be created at the regional level would wish to overleap the national capitals, and deal directly with the authorities in Brussels? As anyone who has watched the skilful lobbying of the Commission by the Scottish Development Agency can testify, this is already beginning to happen, and the more it happens, the more likely it is that ordinary citizens, as well as office holders, in the regions will see Brussels as a counterweight to the existing national capitals. At a deeper and more important level, moreover, the revival of non-state nationalism shows that national loyalties are much less stable than British pragmatists assume. Thirty years ago, Scottish nationalism was a joke. Today it is a force. Today, Breton nationalism, though not exactly a joke, is still a little comic—at any rate, to complacent centralist administrators in Paris. Who knows what will be happening in Brittany thirty years from now? And if the classical nation state has suddenly had to face a rival for its citizens' loyalties in the shape of emergent 'ethnicities' which are not, and in some cases never have been nation states, and which hardly manifested themselves in politics as recently as a generation ago, is it not possible that it may one day have to face a supranational rival as well? If large numbers of Scots no longer feel loyal in the traditional way to the British nation state, partly because they have become increasingly dubious about the capacity of the traditional British state to look after Scottish interests satisfactorily, and partly because they have come to feel increasingly

Scottish as a result, is it not conceivable that they might one day come to the conclusion that their interests can be looked after properly only in 'Europe'? If they come to that conclusion, might they also come to feel 'European' and develop a 'European' loyalty?

Implicit in the British view that the existence of strong national loyalties rules out a supranational Community is an assumption that structure must follow sentiment: that national feelings come first and that the political organisation that embodies those feelings follows later. But this is to take the classical nineteenth-century European nation state at its face value, and in doing so to misread one of the most important chapters of modern European history. In reality, most nineteenth-century nation states were based, to a considerable extent, on bluff. Large parts of France were not French, in sentiment or in language, until well into the nineteenth century. Fierce efforts had to be made by the French central authorities to inculcate French feeling into large parts of the country as late as the Third Republic, and these efforts were not very successful until almost the beginning of the present century.[2] French nationalism did not grow spontaneously from below. It was deliberately planted by the French State, and had to be watered with considerable care. And what is true of France is more obviously true of Italy and Germany. Movements for national unification succeeded in mid-nineteenth-century Germany and Italy—it must be admitted, only with the aid of armed force—despite the existence of profound economic, social and cultural differences which made themselves felt quite strongly as soon as the excitement of unification had worn off. The Italian and German peoples played little part in the process. Italy and Germany were united, not by the spontaneous and irresistible flowering of Italian and German national consciousness, but by small and dedicated élites with bayonets at their backs. After unification, Bavarians came to feel German and Neapolitans Italian. It would be rash to conclude that many had done so before, or that many would have done so afterwards if unification had stopped short at their frontiers. Suppose Bavaria had been left out of Bismarck's Reich, as Austria was. Would the Bavarians now feel more German than the Austrians do? There is no way of telling of course, but, to put it at its lowest, it would be risky to base one's conception of the future of the European Community on the assumption that the only possible answer is 'yes'.

Nationalism was unquestionably a powerful force in nineteenth-century Europe, and is still a powerful force in contemporary Europe. But it was, and remains, a political programme, like Marxism or liberalism, not a sociological fact. The great nationalist historians of the nineteenth century, whose writings still colour men's views of these matters, were propagandists as well as scholars, seeking to inculcate and fortify the national feelings whose histories they told. Their picture of the nation state as the highest and most faithful expression of the social will is as controversial, and as open to doubt, as Marx's picture of the nationless proletariat, or as the classical economists' picture of the beneficent operations of the hidden hand of perfect competition. Its accuracy can be established only by looking at the evidence; and what the evidence shows is that, in some places, the state was there long before the modern conception of nationhood had come into existence and that, in others, new nation states were created in the name of alleged nationalities which played very little part in the process of creating them. It does not show that the nation was there before the state, or that the state had to be created to satisfy the nation. Much the same is true of nationalism today. The question of how much power should be left in the hands of the member Governments of the Community and of how much should be transferred to Community authorities is a matter for debate. It is possible to argue that the nation state is perfectly capable of discharging all the functions it discharges at present, and that no power should be transferred. But that case must be argued on its merits, by reference to the evidence. To claim that it is impossible to transfer significantly more power because national feelings rule it out is to beg a whole series of complicated sociological and political questions, to which no honest man can possibly pretend to know the answer. All that we know is that a certain amount of power has already been transferred, and that in the original Six at any rate, these transfers have encountered no popular opposition whatever.

Public Opinion and Integration

This is not to say that present-day Europe could (or should) be united from above in the way that Germany and Italy were united a hundred years ago. We are now living in mass democracies, in which the ordinary citizen has a much louder voice than his great-grandfather had in the middle of the nineteenth century. But this would be a fatal stumbling block to more supranationalism only if ordinary citizens in the Member States were opposed to it. The evidence suggests that in reality—at any rate, in the original six Member States—the Community is popular and that supranational initiatives would be popular as well.[3] The notion that integration is held up by deep-seated social or cultural differences implies that the Governments would have gone further if only their peoples had let them. To put it at its lowest, this is at least as implausible as the opposite notion that the people of Europe are panting for more integration and are held back only by selfish and short-sighted Governments.

It is true that national Governments—and, even more, national administrations—have frequently frustrated further integration in practice. It is also true that some of the national politicians and officials concerned have suggested that their reason for doing so is that the people for whom they speak would not stomach further integration. But it would be naïve to take such statements at face value. The issues on which national administrations drag their feet are often highly technical and complex, and the ordinary citizen rarely knows much about them. Take, for example, the great struggle between the Commission and the British Government over the introduction of the tachograph in lorry drivers' cabs. British lorry drivers dislike the tachograph because they do not want an unfalsifiable record of their driving practices to be available for inspection. Because of the weight of the lorry drivers in the Transport and General Workers Union, the Union has come out against the tachograph; because of the weight of the union in the Labour Party, the Government has opposed it too. How many British citizens know what the Government has been doing in their name? And how many would agree with it if they knew what the issues are? The truth is that opposition to further integration comes from those who hold power in the national systems which will have to lose power to a Community system if integration is to take place. We do not know whether ordinary citizens agree with their opposition. All that we know is that no one has bothered to find out.

Social, economic and cultural differences exist in present-day Europe, of course. But it is not at all clear that they go any deeper than did the equivalent differences in mid-nineteenth-century Germany or Italy: that a present-day Sicilian, say, would feel less at home in London than his great-grandfather would have felt in Turin, or that a present-day Bavarian would feel less at home in Paris than his great-grandfather would have felt in Berlin. What *is* clear is that the social, economic and cultural differences which divide the Member States of the Community from each other are far less marked today than they were thirty, or even twenty, years ago. Manchester is much closer to Milan, and Bremen to Brest or Naples to Namur, than it was in 1959 or 1949. Yet the movement for European unity, which provided the moral and political basis for the Community, was stronger in 1949 than it is in 1979, while the Community made faster progress towards integration in its early years than it has done recently. The alleged reasons for the Community's failure to fulfil the hopes of the founding fathers are, in short, less significant today than they were a generation ago. Yet progress is slower today than it was then. This suggests that the real reasons for slow progress lie elsewhere.

To be sure, Britain seems to be a special case. In the United Kingdom, the opinion polls suggest that the Community is not popular, and that movements in a supranational direction would not be popular either. When British politicians use the alleged social, cultural and economic differences between Member States as a reason for opposing further integration, they are thinking of Britain, not of the Community as a whole. But Britain is, after all, part of the Community; and if the British people were irredeemably opposed to more integration, a supranational Community would be possible only if Britain were left outside. As we saw in Chapter 1, the differences between

Britain and the continent *are* greater than those between any of the continental countries. It does not follow, however, that the differences constitute an insuperable obstacle to further integration. The only evidence we have of what the British people really think—in a situation in which they were forced to make a choice, instead of grumbling to a canvasser or an opinion pollster—is the result of the Referendum. In the Referendum, the British people voted overwhelmingly, by a far bigger majority than in any general election since the war, for continued membership of the Community. It is true that they did not vote for a supranational Community. But they did not vote against it either. If a referendum were held on monetary union say, or on a strong Community industrial or environmental policy, and the arguments for and against were openly and clearly deployed in the way that the arguments for and against continued membership of the Community were deployed in 1975, the outcome might well be what it was in 1975.

The fact remains, however, that the British seem to be less enthusiastic about belonging to the Community than any other people does; and that that fact has to be explained. One important reason is the way in which the British Government has behaved since the Referendum. If British Ministers had declared unequivocally that the issue was closed when the votes were counted, and had made it clear that they would operate henceforth in the spirit of the Referendum result, public attitudes would almost certainly be very different. Instead, they did exactly the opposite. Some of the most important ministerial offices, so far as day-to-day negotiations with other Community countries are concerned, are held by convinced anti-marketeers. Their interest lies, not in reaching agreements which would benefit their country, but in proving to their own party supporters that they are still faithful to their anti-market principles. This has had two pernicious effects. In the first place, Britain has benefited less from Community membership than she would have done otherwise. Our Community partners have come to regard us at best with dismay, and at worst with suspicion bordering on hostility. They have been less willing to accommodate our special interests than they would have been if we had behaved less intransigently; and because we have won

55

fewer negotiating successes than we would otherwise have done, it has been more difficult to make a pro-European case than it would otherwise have been. Secondly—and perhaps even more perniciously—the Community process has been depicted to the British people as an endless struggle between a collection of selfish continentals, trying to screw the last farthing out of the British Government, and gallant British ministers, saving their country from exploitation only by using all their teeth and claws. To put it at its lowest, this is not a good way to persuade them that membership of the Community is desirable.

The Revival of France and Germany

But only a small part of the blame for the slow progress of recent years lies with the British. By definition, integration entails a transfer of power from national political systems—not just from national Governments, but from national administrations, national political parties, and even from nationally organised interest groups—to a Community system. If an effective Community anti-pollution policy is to be initiated, decisions about the permissible levels of industrial effluent, about smoke control, perhaps about traffic management, will have to be taken, at any rate in part, in Brussels rather than in national capitals. If such a policy is established, interest groups will have to lobby the authorities concerned in Brussels, as well as the authorities with which they are familiar in their own countries; and if they are to operate on a Community level they will have to co-operate with their opposite numbers in the other Member States of the Community, and transfer power from their national headquarters. If the European Parliament acquires a significant role in Community decision-making, Community political parties will develop; and the national parties will have to transfer power from national party head offices to a Community apparatus.

Those who hold power in a national system may be willing to give it up if they think that its loss is inevitable, or that in the long run they will lose more by hanging on to it than by abandoning it. But they rarely like such a prospect, and they have a strong tendency to search for arguments to show that there is no need for them to do anything of the kind.[4] The more deeply entrenched the national system concerned, the more stubborn (and the more successful) their search is likely to be. In the early years of the Community, however, the national systems of the two strongest member states were both much less well-entrenched than they are today. When the Rome Treaty was signed, the Federal Republic was only eight years old. Its institutions were still fragile, and, in the eyes of large numbers of its citizens at any rate, lacking in legitimacy. Only a few years before, the parties had differed sharply and passionately over the fundamentals of foreign policy. The Social Democrats had opposed German re-armament and membership of NATO at the beginning of the decade, hoping that it might be possible to trade unification for neutralisation. The Christian Democrats had won the fight for re-armament and membership of NATO, but they could not be certain that their victory would last. Strong neutralist tendencies could still be detected in the Social Democratic Party, and it was always possible that they might be echoed by German public opinion. There could be no guarantee that if the Soviet Union made some new initiative to detach Germany from the West, offering German unification in return for neutralisation, the S.P.D. would not come out in favour and win an election on that ticket. At another level, the German élite was desperately conscious of the legacy of the war and of the unpopularity and suspicion with which Germany was regarded by her neighbours, and desperately anxious for international acceptance and respectability. For all these reasons the Government was not merely willing, but eager, to join a supranational European Community, which would lock the Federal Republic, irrevocably into the Western world.

The situation in France was different, but the results were similar. The French Fourth Republic was manifestly incapable of solving France's internal or external problems. The French economy was racked by terrible strikes; the Communist-led trade unions were hardly assimilated into the social order; and the parties of the centre, which alone supported the institutions of the Republic, commanded only a transient and insecure majority in the National Assembly. France had emerged from

the war badly shaken, had seen defeat after defeat in Indo-
China, and was beginning to embark on the Algerian War,
having (together with Britain) failed disastrously in the 1956
Suez expedition. Like the Germans, though for different reasons,
the French élite saw Europe as a way of escaping from its
internal problems.

None of this is true today. The Federal Republic is one of
the stablest and most successful regimes in the world. The
French Fifth Republic can legitimately boast that it has made
France more prosperous relatively to other countries, and more
influential politically, than she has been, perhaps since the time
of Napoleon III, and certainly since the 1920s. To be sure,
Britain's national system is considerably less well-entrenched
than it was twenty years ago. The British ruling élite has lost
self-confidence; there are strong separatist movements in Wales
and Scotland; the political system is coming under increasing
criticism and the economic record is one of almost uninter-
rupted failure. But twenty years ago, after all, Britain's national
system was so well entrenched that those who ran it were unwill-
ing to join the Community at all. It is still well enough entrenched to constitute a formidable obstacle to further integration. In Italy, and most of the smaller Member States, the
inadequacies of the classical nation state are still obvious. The
Italian political class is deeply uncertain of its ability to handle
the country's increasingly intractable social and economic
problems. Europe still beckons to it—in the sort of way that it
beckoned to the French in the 1950s—as a solution to internal
problems. The Luxemburgers, the Belgians and even the Dutch
know that they have no hope of influencing world affairs, and
only a scant hope of influencing European affairs, on their own.
For them supranationalism is the only alternative to impotence.
The same applies, even more forcibly, to the Irish, to whom
membership offers the only possible escape from the age-old,
long-hated embrace of London. Indeed, Denmark is the only
small Member State where the Community does not seem to
be popular—perhaps understandably since Denmark joined
only just before the oil crisis and therefore tends to blame
membership of the Community for the evils which inevitably
ensued. Italy and the smaller countries do not, however, deter-

mine the fate of the Community. What matters is that in the three strongest Member States the inadequacies of the classical nation state are masked, either by the regime's success, as in Germany and France, or by the incompleteness of its failure, as in the United Kingdom.

Popular attitudes have changed as well. When the Rome Treaty was signed, the peoples of Europe were still living in the shadow of the Second World War. Memories of defeat, occupation, and the humiliation and despair that accompanied them, were still vivid. The case for integration is based on two fundamental assumptions — that unbridled nationalism leads to disaster, and that the classical European nation state is no longer capable of safeguarding the interests of its people. Both seemed almost self-evident to millions of Europeans twenty years ago. Today attitudes are a good deal more complicated. There is still great popular support for the Community, and indeed for supranationalism. But there is little grass-roots pressure for it. At another level, it is important to remember that in the 1950s Europe was still a dream. Today it is part of the landscape, and a rather hum-drum part at that. Then, again, the Community's very success has eroded popular enthusiasm. In the immediate post-war period, there was a strong sense of crisis. New Europeans have got used to prosperity. Few under the age of 50 can imagine how desperate was Europe's plight in the 1940s and early 1950s before the Community came into existence; few over 50 can remember. Meanwhile, the nation state has become better at dealing with its social and economic problems. Its citizens are much more likely to see their national Governments as the providers of benefits than they were twenty years ago, and correspondingly less anxious to see power transferred to the Community.

The Technocratic Fallacy

For all these reasons, the climate for integration is considerably colder than it was when the Treaty was signed. Unfortunately, however, the institutional structure created by the Treaty has turned out to be ill-suited to the cold. Central to the whole

Monnet system—central, indeed, to Monnet's personal view of the world—was an implicit assumption that politics could be banished from the process of integration. For Monnet was a technocrat par excellence—the most impressive example of the species, perhaps, in modern Europe. As he tells in his memoirs he thought of entering politics at a high level in France after the war, but did not, because he found the life of politics distasteful.[5] He was an ambitious man, who enjoyed getting things done, and delighted in the exercise of power, but he had no ideological affiliations and no interest in ideology. Running through his memoirs is a strong note of impatience at the propensity of politicians to waste time arguing about theological questions with which no serious man would bother, and an even stronger note of impatience with the propensity of political parties to put their own special interests above the good of the whole. These attitudes were fortified by his experience in postwar France, when he headed the a-political Commissariat Général du Plan, created very much in his own personal image to modernise France. When he transferred his energies from the national to the European level, he brought the same attitudes with him. It seemed to him that, just as France could be modernised by the a-political expertise of a technocratic Commissariat Général, so Europe could be united by the a-political expertise of a technocratic High Authority, whose proposals would carry weight, not because of the representative character of their authors, but because of their intrinsic technical merits. Integration was clearly in everyone's interests; the obstacles to it were technical, not political. It followed that there would be no need to exert political pressure or to fight political battles in order to achieve it. In so far as political skills were needed at all, they were the skills of the corridor politician, not of the mass leader. And what was most needed was disinterested expertise.

At first, these assumptions seemed to have been vindicated. The Coal and Steel Community was a triumphant success; Euratom and the Economic Community were duly created in its image. The tariff barriers came down and living standards shot up; for a while, even the French Gaullists seemed incapable of swimming with real conviction against such a beneficent tide. In the end however the tide turned, for the reasons we have been discussing; and we can now see that the Monnet system was based on a false premise after all.

For, in reality, the important obstacles to integration are not technical at all, even though they are often camouflaged in technicalities. They are political. To overcome them, political pressures do have to be exerted, and political battles fought. The opposition of particular vested interests can be overcome only by mobilising the whole—just as in a single nation state public opinion has to be mobilised in support of policies which are clearly in the national interest but contrary to the sectional interest of particular groups. As things are, however, no institution in the Community can do this. Under the Treaties, it is the Commission—and only the Commission—which has to provide the impetus for integration. If the Commission fails to provide it, no one else can do so instead. Not only does the Commission have a monopoly of the right of initiative, but the Commission is the only institution which has both a significant role in the decision-making process, and a European as opposed to a national mandate. The European Parliament, which also has a European mandate, plays little part in the decision-making process; the Council of Ministers has a national and not a European mandate, and a national rather than a European view. To be sure, important initiatives have sometimes been taken by the Heads of Government assembled in the European Council. But the European Council is a sort of *deus ex machina*, which descends occasionally from the clouds to break a log-jam in Community affairs. By its very nature, it cannot be a continuous presence, constantly pushing the Community forward.

In spite of its crucial role in the process of integration, however, the Commission of the 1970s is only the old, a-political High Authority of the 1950s, writ, if anything, slightly small. It cannot provide enough impetus to overcome the resistance which is bound to come from the national institutions whose power is threatened by integration, since it cannot exert pressure or engage, with any hope of victory, in political battles with member Governments. In the Western world, at any rate, the source of political authority is popular election. National

Governments, responsible to elected parliaments, possess not only the sword of power but the sceptre of democratic legitimacy. The Commission possesses neither. It has highly political functions, but no political base. Commissioners behave (and are behaved to) as though they were members of a responsible Government. They hobnob, on more or less equal terms, with national ministers. They answer questions and reply to debates in the European Parliament, for all the world like real ministers in a real parliament. Their President is received by heads of state, and takes part in meetings of the European Council alongside national prime ministers. But all this is make-believe. Sometimes, some Commissioners have had distinguished political careers before coming to the Commission, but in their capacities as members of the Commission they are peculiarly grand *hauts fonctionnaires*, not politicians. They are elected by no one and represent no one. Their authority, which is often considerable, is personal, not representative: technical, not political.[6]

These handicaps do not prevent the Commission from playing a central role in Community affairs. The Commission acts as a kind of honest broker between the Member States. Its officials are better placed to win the trust of national officials than are the officials of any one Member State. Often, it is the Commission which puts forward the compromise which finally breaks a log-jam in the Council of Ministers. For the same reason, the Commission plays an important part in international negotiations—a good example being the north-south conference in Paris in 1957. It is also the chief manager of existing Community policies. Finally, and perhaps most importantly of all, the Commission acts as a sort of European think-tank. Since it, and it alone, has both a European mandate and the expertise to develop policies on European matters, it constantly puts forward suggestions for the future evolution of the Community, which become the stuff of discussion in national capitals and eventually in the Council of Ministers. These three roles—as honest broker, manager and thinker—are undoubtedly of critical importance to the Community. But although it is sometimes suggested that the Commission's ability to play them depends precisely on the fact that it is not obliged constantly to peer over its shoulder at public opinion or vested interests, and that its lack of a political base is therefore a source of strength, the suggestion betrays considerable confusion of thought. Bodies which appeal to public opinion are not thereby obliged to think only in short-term ways. It is, indeed, indispensable for the Community that a body with a purely European mandate and a purely European view, as opposed to a national mandate and a national view, should play a central part in the decision-making process. The Commission's role could not be played by a secretariat controlled by member Governments. But the Commission's European mandate does not derive from the fact that it lacks a political base. In any event, the Commission was not set up merely to act as a manager, thinker and honest broker. It was set up to be 'the motor of integration'. It has become clear that that role cannot be played successfully by a body which, by its very nature, speaks for no one but itself.

It is true that the Commission has established relations with a number of organised interest groups—quaintly described as 'Social Partners'—throughout the Community. It is sometimes suggested that it does not need a political base as well: that the way to build Europe is to by-pass the traditional political forces and engage the interests instead: even that the existing institutional structure is ideally suited to that task. But although the Commission is engaged in a continuous flurry of negotiation, collaboration and consultation, not only with interest groups but with national administrations as well, these links in no way counterbalance the national Governments' collective monopoly of democratic legitimacy. In a fight with a Member State it is not much use the Commission saying that it has had close consultations with an organised lobby if the member Government can speak in the name of the whole of its people. Organised interest groups, moreover, have only partial views of the European interest. Their views can cut across national frontiers, but they are no more capable of considering the interests of the Community as a whole than is any single member Government.

The Commission's lack of legitimacy, moreover, inhibits it from making serious attempts to mobilise public opinion behind its proposals. On issue after issue—aero-space, the environment, energy—public opinion might be mobilised in favour of supranational policies if someone tried to mobilise it. Yet the Commission has made only the most fitful and half-hearted attempts to do so. Part of the reason, no doubt, is political cowardice. So long as Commissioners depend for their appointment on national Governments, and for their future careers on their future acceptability to national Governments, they are bound to be reluctant to lead public opinion into battle against national Governments. But that provides only part of the explanation. A much more important factor is that the Commission — whether brave or cowardly — always faces a conflict between the possible and the desirable. If it leads public opinion against a member Government, it is likely to exasperate the member Government concerned, and it will find it that much more difficult to get its proposals through the Council of Ministers. If Roy Jenkins were to launch a campaign against the Callaghan government on the tachograph question, he might win the battle for British public opinion, but his reward would be less, not more, support from the British Government on other important issues. The problem would still exist even if the Commission had a political base. But it would loom much less large in Commissioners' minds.

The Democratic Deficit

As things are at present, moreover, there are also strong arguments of democratic principle against transferring power from the national to the Community level in the way which has been advocated here. There can be no democracy without accountability. In a democratic system someone must always be in a position to use Harry Truman's motto, 'the buck stops here'; decision-makers must be answerable to, and removable by, those in whose name the decisions are made. In the Community system, no one is unambiguously answerable for anything. The buck is never seen to stop; it is hidden from view, in an endless scrimmage of consultation and bargaining. This may not matter much when the Community's competences are as restricted as they are at present. If they were extended sufficiently to overcome the challenges described above, it would matter a great deal. Monetary union, as we have seen, would entail taking two critically important instruments of economic management out of national hands and putting them into Community hands. National Governments would still be able to decide the level and composition of public expenditure and of taxation, but the monetary framework within which these decisions were taken would be laid down at the centre. National institutions would still make their own trade-offs between wage increases and unemployment, but a Member State with a high propensity to wage inflation could no longer devalue its currency against other Community currencies. The decisions taken at Community level would thus be of enormous political importance, and the body taking them would have to be subject to responsible political direction and control. And, as we have seen, none of the existing Community institutions is capable of providing this.

Similar considerations apply to majority voting in the Council of Ministers. This would greatly increase the Commission's power without making it more accountable to anyone. Control by national parliaments over the activities of the Council of Ministers would be undermined. So long as each Member Government can veto a Council decision, if it wants to, there is a sense in which each Member Government is responsible for all Council decisions, and can therefore be held to account for them by its Parliament. If national vetoes disappear this will no longer be true; and a national Parliament will no longer be able to hold its Government to account for what the Council has done. The resulting 'democratic deficit' would not be acceptable in a Community committed to democratic principles. Yet such a deficit would be inevitable unless the gap were somehow to be filled by the European Parliament.

Thus the Community is caught in an *impasse*. If it does not move forward, it is almost certain to slide back. But it cannot move forward—should not, indeed, be allowed to move forward—so long as the motive force has to come from an unrepresentative technocracy with no popular mandate or popular base, and so long as there is no machinery to make the Community's decision-makers accountable at Community level to the elected representatives of the people. It follows that the Commission is caught in an *impasse* too. For if the Commission is to provide the motive force which the Community needs it will somehow have to acquire the democratic legitimacy which it has lacked hitherto. It can do this only if it is prepared to give up some of its most cherished prerogatives and change some of its most deeply-held attitudes.

4

Direct Elections: Opportunities and Dangers

The European elections due later this year should be considered against the background sketched out in the last chapter. Will they help to correct the institutional imbalance which lies at the heart of the stagnation in Community affairs? Will they help to fill the 'democratic deficit' which would result from majority voting in the Council of Ministers if the existing mechanisms of parliamentary control were left unchanged? Will they make it possible to create a monetary union without violating the fundamental principles of democratic accountability?

These questions cannot be answered with complete confidence until we know who the Members of the directly elected Parliament are, and what expectations and ambitions they bring with them. A Parliament of ageing party warhorses put out to grass would clearly be a different proposition from a Parliament of sharp and ambitious young Turks; a Parliament with a Socialist-Communist majority might not behave in a way that would be considered appropriate by a Parliament with a right-centre majority. Even before the composition of the Parliament is known, however, some points can be established and some guesses made. In the first place, it seems clear that direct elections will increase Parliament's weight. Secondly, it seems clear that they will increase its appetite. Thirdly, it seems likely that these two effects will create a series of problems for the Community, about which there has so far been little public discussion. Fourthly, however, it seems clear that—provided the problems are properly understood and handled with good sense —the combination of added parliamentary weight and increased parliamentary appetite will, at any rate, give the Community a better chance of escaping from the *impasse* described in chapter 3 than it has ever had before.

It is true that some national Parliaments, at any rate, will be watching jealously to make sure that the European Parliament does not gain power at their expense. In Britain and France, the legislation making it possible to hold direct elections contained explicit provisions to prevent the European Parliament from increasing its power without the approval of the Westminster Parliament and the National Assembly respectively; and it is not likely that the French and British Governments will change their attitudes at all quickly. In both countries, however, the debate on the powers of the European Parliament was as ill-informed as it was inward-looking. It was conducted on the tacit assumption that the only way in which the European Parliament can gain power is to take it away from national Parliaments. That assumption is quite false. There are, in fact, at least three ways in which the European Parliament might gain power, not one. If the Community's competences were extended in a field in which the Parliament already has a say in decision-making, Parliament would automatically gain power as a result. If the Regional Fund were doubled in size, for example, the European Parliament would automatically gain power, since expenditure on the Regional Fund falls into the category of Community spending over which the European Parliament has the last word. If the Community were given new functions in a field in which the European Parliament has no power at present, the Parliament would nevertheless gain power if the decision to transfer that function to the Community were accompanied by a decision to give Parliament a say in the way in which it is exercised. An example might be a decision to set up a new Community monetary authority, and to make that authority accountable to the European Parliament. Finally, the European Parliament could acquire new powers over functions which are already exercised by the Community—for example, over the operation of the common agricultural policy. Only the second of these would almost always entail losses of power on the part of national Parliaments, and even that would not invariably do so.

The truth is that a large range of important decisions is now taken at Community level, by a process which is almost free of any parliamentary scrutiny or control. The only national Parliament which has more than nominal control over its ministers' activities in the Council of Ministers is the Danish Folketing; and even the Folketing is powerless to scrutinise them, since the Market Relations Committee which exercises the control function meets in private and is debarred from divulging its proceedings to the Folketing at large.[1] The system is, in fact, a kind of parliamentary oligarchy, in which the ordinary members of the Folketing play no part. In any case, no other Community Government shows the remotest sign of imitating the Danish system.[2] If the European Parliament were to acquire a say in the activities of the Council, and establish machinery by which some of those activities were opened up to public scrutiny, the quantum of parliamentary power in the Community would be increased at no cost to the power of any national Parliament.

The same applies to the relationship between the European Parliament and the Commission. The Commission is not, and cannot be, answerable to any national Parliament, for the obvious reason that it is not a national body; and as the scrutiny committees of the British Parliament have discovered, it takes great care to make that clear in its dealings with national Parliaments. The only Parliament which can possibly scrutinise or control the Commission is the European Parliament. The European Parliament exercises those functions already, but patchily and ineffectively; and, as a result, the Commission is much more free of parliamentary control than any bureaucracy ought to be. The European Parliament could (and indeed should) acquire considerably more power over the Commission; and if it did so, it would increase its own powers without curtailing the powers of any national Parliament. Indeed, one might even conceive of a *de facto* alliance between the European Parliament and at any rate some national Parliaments, by which the European Parliament would seek more power at Community level, and would receive support from national Parliaments, because the latter recognised that this was the only way to strengthen the democratic element in Community decision-making.

The widely held notion that the European Parliament's powers cannot be increased in the foreseeable future is therefore oversimplified. And whatever happens to its powers, there can be no doubt that the mere fact of being elected will give its Members considerably more moral authority than the nominated Members possess at present. The national Governments' collective monopoly of democratic legitimacy will at last have been broken. On Community matters, at any rate, the Parliament will have more right to speak in the name of the sovereign people than have the representatives of the member Governments sitting in the Council of Ministers. There can be no question that this is one of the biggest steps forward in the Community's history.

A European Political Class?

Increased weight is certain. Increased appetite is not certain, but it is highly likely. In the first place, the elected Parliament will have a much larger proportion of full-time European politicians among its 410 members than the nominated Parliament has among its 198. It is true that the so-called 'dual mandate' will continue, and that in some Member States, a significant proportion of the directly elected Members will still belong to a national Parliament as well. As time goes on, however, it is virtually certain that Members of the European Parliament with a dual mandate will have to choose whether to put their European or their national commitments first. The directly elected Parliament is almost certain to generate far more work for its Members than the present Parliament generates, and even now it cannot cope adequately with the work it is supposed to do.[3] Members with a dual mandate will find it impossible in practice to discharge both their obligations to their national Parliaments and their obligations to the European

Parliament. No doubt, some will choose the national Parliament, and will make only rare and fleeting appearances at Strasbourg and Luxembourg. Others will choose the European Parliament, for the same complicated set of reasons which already lead some nominated Members to make the European Parliament rather than the national Parliament the main focus of their activities. And, of course, some Members will have only a single mandate. There will therefore be a considerable number of *de facto* European politicians in search of a role, anxious to prove to themselves and to others that they are doing something useful.

For the Members of the European Parliament will have been elected, and, in most cases at any rate, they will presumably wish to be re-elected. If they are to have any hope of re-election, they will have to justify themselves to their constituents, if they have identifiable constituents, and in any case to their parties. One of their main concerns will be to bring the Community down to earth: to show ordinary voters what the Community means, what decisions are taken at Community level, and what an important part the European Member plays in influencing the decisions taken at Community level. Directly elected Members will also want to justify their existences to themselves. Politicians usually wish to influence events, and European policitians will wish to influence European events. Self respect, as well as self interest, will impel them into a search for influence and power. Once the European Parliament is directly elected, moreover, lobbies and pressure groups all over the Community are likely to regard it as a useful focus for activity. As any Member of the House of Commons quickly learns, one of the primary engines of parliamentary activity is pressure-group activity. Members of Parliament press for things to be done, in part, at any rate, because they are themselves subject to pressure from bodies and individuals outside. The more outside bodies and individuals think it is worth while to bring pressure to bear on Members of the European Parliament, the more pressure the European Parliament will bring to bear on the Commission and the Council. Finally, it is, at any rate, possible that political parties in the Member States will sometimes behave in the same way. A party which has been defeated in a national election might well try to use the European Parliament as a stick with which to beat its successful rival at home. If the Conservatives were to lose the next General Election in Britain, the Conservative Group at Strasbourg would have no inhibitions about building up the European Parliament, and might even see domestic political advantages in doing so. Odd though it may seem at present, the same might be true of Labour Members of the European Parliament if the Labour Party lost office at Westminster.

This picture of a virile and assertive Parliament, reaching out for ways of influencing Community decisions and for ways of proving to the electorate that it is capable of influencing them, rests of course, on the assumption that its Members will be politically virile and assertive people. That assumption is sometimes challenged. It is sometimes said that the directly elected Parliament will not seek more influence—or, at any rate, that it will not be able to gain more influence—because its Members will not be adequate to such demanding tasks. The directly elected Members, it is sometimes said, will consist of has-beens and never-will-bes: of what a senior Member of the Commission once described to the present writer as 'retired colonels and worthy non-commissioned officers'. Hence, it is said, Utopian dreams about the effect of direct elections on the Community's decision-making process will break down in practice. The great men of Europe—the Brandts, the Heaths, the Mitterrands, the Callaghans, the Schmidts, and the would-be Heaths, Callaghans and Schmidts—will still want to make their careers at the national level, and will still tower over the puny figures who decide to operate primarily at Strasbourg and Luxembourg.

A second sceptical prediction is that direct elections will have the paradoxical, even perverse, effect of making the European Parliament more nationalistic, and at the same time more parochial, than the present Parliament is. The nominated Parliament, after all, is largely composed of self-selected 'good Europeans'. These tend, naturally and instinctively, to side with the the Commission against the Council, and to put 'Europe' first, and their national interests second. But, say the proponents of this view, they are able to do this only because they are not elected, and have no need to fear a constituency. Their voters at home are sublimely ignorant of what Euro-Members do at Strasbourg and Luxembourg, and do not realise that their alleged representatives are behaving in such an unrepresentative fashion. Direct elections will change all this. The directly elected Members will have to be far more responsive to local pressures than the nominated ones have been if they are to survive. But these local pressures will not be *communautaire* in character. If anything, they will be *anti-communautaire*. Local interests will be fighting for a bigger share of the pork barrel. They will not be concerned with the fate of the Community as a whole. Directly elected Members may see themselves initially as the part-architects of a new and better Europe. They will soon discover that they are expected to act as the spokesmen for the parish pump—and not only for the parish pump but for the national pump as well.

The first of these sceptical predictions rests on the assumption that the Community's political talent is at present monopolised by the national Parliaments and the national parties. It is, of course, a widely-held assumption, particularly among members of national Parliaments, professional watchers of national Parliaments, and would-be members and watchers of national Parliaments; and since these three groups added together account for a large proportion of the most vocal members of the political class in any Member State, it often goes almost unchallenged. But that does not make it true. Even in the highly centralised United Kingdom, where local government has little freedom of action, a great deal of political talent—much of it far more impressive than the talent at Westminster—is to be found at local level. For obvious reasons, this is much more true of Federal Germany. Both Brandt and Schmidt, it should be remembered, made their reputations as Land politicians, not as Federal ones. So, for that matter, did Adenauer—though admittedly in an earlier period of German history.

Why should the same thing not happen at the Community level? Why should ambitious and aspiring politicians not regard membership of the European Parliament as a sensible and worthwhile way of furthering their political careers? Why should it be taken for granted that membership of a national

Parliament, whose power and influence are fixed and circum-
scribed, is bound to be more rewarding than membership of
the European Parliament, whose power and influence can only
increase? Why should a career spent trying to build a united
and democratic Europe not seem more fulfilling, at any rate to
politicians with intelligence and imagination, than a career of
propping up a decaying national structure which has served
its purpose? Why, in short, should the future not beckon at
least as enticingly as the past?

Most (though by no means all) able and established national
politicians will, no doubt, prefer to remain in national politics.
But it is worth remembering that when regimes change—when
the French Fourth Republic gave way to the Fifth, for example,
or when the British political landscape was transformed by
total war—new men almost invariably appear on the scene and
that the new men are often abler than the old. The political
class in Fifth Republic France overlaps to some extent with the
political class of the Fourth Republic, but only to some extent.
Mitterrand was a Minister in the Fourth Republic, but where
was Michel Roccard? And where were Pompidou and Giscard
d'Estaing? The same was true of Britain in the 1920s and the
1940s. Large numbers of able young men entered politics as
Labour M.P.s in 1945, many of them without pre-war political
experience, or pre-war political ambition. A whole army of
talented new men appeared in the House of Commons in 1922
and 1923 as Labour Members, most of whom had been completely obscure before 1914. One of the most dangerous mistakes
a politician or political analyst can make is that made by Lord
Randolph Churchill when he 'forgot Goschen'. Obscure has-
beens and apparent never-will-bes can achieve greatness, or
have greatness thrust upon them, if the circumstances are
appropriate. Who had heard of Oliver Cromwell before the
Long Parliament met? Who had heard of Robespierre in 1788?

Direct Elections and the Parish Pump

The alleged threat of parish-pump politics raises more complicated considerations. The directly elected Parliament will

almost certainly be more anxious to push local, and in some cases even national, interests than the nominated Parliament has been. It can hardly fail to be more responsive to the wishes of ordinary voters, and more anxious to display its responsiveness. But it would be a great mistake to assume that parochialism, or even nationalism, is necessarily incompatible with Europeanism. As anyone who has ever played any part in politics soon realises, roles influence their players. The old French saying that there is more in common between two Deputies, one of whom is a Communist, than between two Communists, one of whom is a Deputy, can apply to European as well as to national politics. Parliaments are even better at indoctrinating their members with their own norms than are public schools or miners' lodges, as a whole long list of angry firebrands who later mellowed into sage and gradualist parliamentary statesmen bears witness. And the norms of the European Parliament are, and will remain, European norms.

Its whole structure and *modus operandi*, moreover, are such that Members who pursue exclusively local or national interests, and refuse to make compromises with their colleagues from other countries, will be isolated and impotent. Unlike the House of Commons, but like most continental Parliaments, it works by consensus rather than by dissensus. The way to make a reputation at Westminster is to make partisan speeches on the floor of the House and ask partisan questions at Question Time; an ability to work easily with Members from the opposite party in a Select Committee counts for little. In the European Parliament, it is the other way round. Speeches in the hemicycle are of little significance; Question Time is an alien, and badly assimilated, Anglo-Saxon import, dominated by the British Members, whose aggressive Westminster habits are apt to seem loutish and ill-mannered to their continental colleagues. What counts is committee work; and the Committees are all multi-national—as, of course, are the three main party groups. Partly because of this structure and partly because it is in any case extraordinarily difficult for a reasonably gregarious and open-minded human being to belong to any institution for any length of time without absorbing it least some of its values and assumptions, the British Labour anti-marketeers who entered the European Parliament in 1975 nearly all ceased to be anti-marketeers in anything but name within a year or two. It is true that they did not all publicise their changes of heart to their colleagues at Westminster, but, with one exception, their behaviour at Strasbourg and Luxembourg showed scarcely any traces of their original anti-market positions. Two former anti-marketeers — Lord Bruce of Donington and John Prescott, the leader of the Labour group — played leading parts in the work of the Parliament, of a remarkably constructive kind. Such influences are likely to make themselves felt even more strongly after direct elections than before.

No doubt, the directly elected Members will be more sensitive to the European interests of their voters, and more anxious to display that sensitivity in public, than their nominated predecessors have been. But it would be a great mistake to jump to the conclusion that the directly elected Parliament will therefore be less *communautaire* than the present Parliament is. American Congressmen have never been slow to promote the interests of their constituents, and by promoting them they have helped to knit the Union together. If the nineteenth-century Senate and House of Representatives had consisted exclusively of high-minded proponents of the federal ideal, who never thrust their hands into the pork barrel or tried to obtain favours for their constituents at home, the United States would have been much slower to develop than it actually was. In fact, of course, nineteenth-century American politics revolved, to a considerable extent, around a competition between vested interests for access to the levers of federal power.[4] But it was this which made ordinary Americans appreciate that they had a stake in the success of the Union. The neo-functionalist theorists of integration, who provided much of the intellectual under-pinning of the activities of the High Authority in the Coal and Steel Community, were well aware of this. The 'founding fathers' recognised that the Community would have to be rooted in interest if it were to develop successfully, and they did their best to ensure that national interest groups became accustomed to operating supranationally as well. One of the reasons why progress towards a supranational Community has been so slow is that this insight has been only partially realised, and that interests are still articulated largely at the national level.

For although the interests of almost all Community citizens have a European as well as a national dimension, most Community citizens are not aware of this. A precondition of further integration is that they should be made aware; and one of the most important tasks of the directly elected Parliament will be to do precisely that. But it will not be able to perform that function if it consists solely of genteel yes-men, who are so anxious to demonstrate their European faith that they forget the electors who sent them there. What is needed is a rough and demanding Parliament, in which the interests of ordinary voters and groups of voters all over the Community are articulated strongly and convincingly, and which thereby brings the Community and the parish pump closer together. The Parliament of a living Community should be a sounding board for the living social and economic forces in the Member States; and the more energetically and forcefully its Members press the demands of the constituents they represent, the better a sounding board it will be. One of the chief weaknesses of the present, nominated Parliament is precisely that it is too remote from the parish pump. One of the chief reasons why those who want to see a more supranational Community should welcome direct elections is that the directly elected Parliament will almost certainly be less remote.

Direct Elections and Integration

Granted that direct elections will add considerably to Parliament's weight and appetite, will increased parliamentary weight and appetite make it easier to achieve further integration? This is a much more complicated question, and the answer to it is more complicated too. In Community circles, it has sometimes been suggested—in terms implying that the suggestion is virtually self-evident—that integration is bound to benefit, since the mere holding of direct elections will in some way 'legitimise' the Community and the Community process. The Patijn Report claimed that direct elections to the European

Parliament 'would ... lend to the exercise of power by the Communities a *legitimacy* which has hitherto been lacking'. The Tindemans Report said that direct elections would 'reinforce the *democratic legitimacy* of the whole European institutional apparatus'.[5] The truth is more disturbing. The suggestion that direct elections are bound to make integration easier founders on the simple fact that the body which is to be elected—namely the Parliament—plays only a trivial role in the integration process. Parliament will indeed gain legitimacy from direct elections. But the institutions which determine what happens in the Community—namely, the Commission and the Council—will not be affected one way or the other. Direct elections will make a difference to the process of integration, and to the legitimacy of the Community as such, only if Parliament's new weight can somehow be brought to bear in favour of integration, and against the resistance of the national institutions whose positions are threatened by integration. There is no guarantee that this will happen. Indeed, it cannot happen unless the Community's present institutional structure is radically changed. For the hard fact is that, as things are at present, Parliament cannot bring any significant influence to bear on the national resistance to integration.

Indeed, if the present institutional structure remains intact, direct elections may make it even more difficult to achieve further integration than it is already. For the reasons discussed above, elected Members are almost certain to want to prove to their constituents and to themselves that they can influence Community decisions. They will soon discover that their influence is very limited. Though the European Parliament has certain powers over Community spending—described in more detail in the next chapter—it has no power over Community revenue-raising. Its role in the legislative process, though not as negligible as is sometimes assumed in the United Kingdom, is merely consultative. Community legislation is proposed by the Commission and decided by the Council; though the Council consults Parliament, Parliament's opinion is not binding. The elaborate process of consultation in which the Commission engages before it makes proposals is not subject to parliamentary scrutiny. Nor are the weekly meetings of the powerful

Committee of Permanent Representatives—normally known as COREPER after its acronym in French—which consists of the nine Ambassadors of the Member States to the Community, acting as a kind of legislative sieve, which sends controversial proposals through to the Council of Ministers, but holds back uncontroversial ones for decision by the Ambassadors themselves. In spheres unconnected with legislation or finance, Parliament's role is even more limited. In spite of the Community's growing importance as a negotiating *bloc*, Parliament plays no part in foreign-policy co-ordination—though its Political Affairs Committee has regular meetings with the foreign minister who holds the presidency of the Council—and does not have to approve the Community's line in trade negotiations. Direct elections will not change any of this. The elected Members will find that laboriously worked-out reports and eloquent speeches in the hemicycle produce no more results than they do at present. Some may sink back into frustrated apathy, but the ablest, the most energetic and the most ambitious can be expected to look for a scapegoat.

The obvious scapegoat will be the Commission. After all, the easiest way for a Member of Parliament to make a reputation is to attack whatever bureaucracy is closest to hand. In the case of European Members, the closest bureaucracy to hand will still be the Commission—a plump and appetising sitting duck for parliamentary marksmen, with little experience of parliamentary ways and, on the whole, a distinctly provocative conception of Parliament's place in the scheme of things. For the Commission's attitude to Parliament is ambivalent. In principle it is all for a strong and vigorous Parliament, capable of playing an important part in Community life. In practice, most Commissioners find attendance at parliamentary debates a tedious chore, to be evaded if it is humanly possible; give such a low priority to answering parliamentary questions that only around half the written questions tabled are answered in the allotted period; and resist all suggestions that they should spend more of their time at parliamentary committees.[6] These attitudes may change after direct elections, of course. But they are unlikely to change quickly, since they reflect the realities of Community power, which will be the same after direct elections as before.

Commissioners dislike having to listen and reply to parliamentary debates because they know that parliamentary debates make little difference to what happens in the Community, and because they prefer to spend their time in more productive ways. A Commissioner's chief task, after all, is to get his proposals through the Council of Ministers. Parliamentary support is an asset to him, but not an important asset; and if he has to choose between courting a powerless Parliament and courting a powerful national Minister or official, he will always choose the latter. No doubt, there will be a honeymoon in Commission-Parliament relations immediately after direct elections, but it is unlikely to last long unless these power relationships change. Unless positive steps are taken to prevent them, clashes between the directly elected Parliament and the Commission are therefore not merely possible, but probable.

It would be wrong to suggest that the Community is bound to suffer if Parliament behaves more aggressively to the Commission. As we have seen, the Commission has many defects. In spite of its small size, it is absurdly cumbersome and bureaucratic; one of the reasons is that it is not subject to adequate parliamentary scrutiny and control. Harold Wilson pointed out some time ago that the Community badly needs an equivalent of the British Public Accounts Committee, capable of striking terror into the hearts of Commission officialdom and of roasting recalcitrant Directors-General in public session. The Budget Committee has now set up a control sub-committee with some of those functions, but it is a pale shadow of its Westminster counterpart. If the elected Parliament makes its control over the Commission more of a reality and less of a constitutional fiction, that will be all to the good. But although the Community would not suffer if Parliament saw itself less as the Commission's poodle, and more as a watchdog over the Commission, it would suffer a great deal if the political energies generated by direct elections were wholly absorbed in futile squabbles between the two institutions. With all its faults, the Commission is the best 'motor of integration' the Community has, and it will not produce much movement if it has to spend its time warding off attacks from frustrated parliamentarians looking for someone to kick.

Yet, as things are at present, it is the only target which frustrated parliamentarians can reach. For Parliament's powers are not only meagre; they are wrongly focused. The only body over which it has any control is the Commission. Though the Council of Ministers is the real centre of power in the Community system, it is not answerable to Parliament. Indeed, it cannot be, since the Ministers who compose it are necessarily answerable to their national Parliaments instead. However strongly Parliament may wish to kick the Council, it has no means of doing so. It has to kick at the Commission instead, and hope that the Member Governments will understand the message — a fact which recently led the Conservative Group to table a motion censuring the Commission on the strange, but understandable, grounds that pressure from the *Council* had 'forced' it to adopt a policy of which the Conservatives disapproved.[7] If no steps are taken to give the elected Parliament a better lever to influence Community decisions, such tactics are likely to be used more and more frequently in future. Unfortunately, however, they will do more damage to the supporters of integration than to its opponents. There may be no alternative, of course; and if there is no alternative, Parliament would be better advised to employ them than to acquiesce indefinitely in its present role. But they would be a poor way to push the Community forward.

Two Contradictions

All this, moreover, is merely a symptom of a profound contradiction, which lies at the heart of the whole institutional structure. At present, it is hidden and implicit, but direct elections will bring it out in the open. The Community system is largely based on the functionalist conception of integration, which became predominant in the early 1950s, when it looked as though the federalism of the 1940s had failed. For the federalists, integration had been a political process, to be achieved by political methods. They had thought in terms of persuading public opinion, of mobilising political forces, of creating political structures. Implicitly, at least, they had assumed that the way

81

to unite Europe was to hold elections to a European Constituent Assembly, which would proceed to draw up a constitution for a European Federation. The functionalists also thought that the eventual goal was political, but for them, the means were technical. Integration would be achieved by demonstrating its technical advantages; when it was achieved in one field, it would 'spill over', inexorably and inevitably, into neighbouring fields. There was no need to engage public opinion or to mobilise political support. Hence, the Community process was to consist, in essence, of a dialogue between the technicians in the Commission and the representatives of national Governments in the Council of Ministers, with no public participation. The European Parliament was a decorative afterthought, added to the building because the architects feared that its design might otherwise be unpopular. Yet, in adding it, the architects implicitly accepted—or at any rate made an important concession to—a quite different, more political, at least quasi-federalist, conception of what integration was about. For there is no point in setting up an institution which has nothing to do; and what Parliaments do is to reflect political opinion and give expression to political demands. The logic of the decision to create the European Parliament, in short, ran counter to the logic underlying the rest of the system. Functionalism had triumphed, but it had been denied—or half-denied—at the moment of its triumph.

This contradiction has not mattered much over the last quarter of a century, since Parliament has had too little weight to play more than a decorative role. After direct elections, however, it will matter a great deal. For the decision to hold direct elections only makes sense on the assumption that the general public ought, in some sense or other, to be represented in Community decision-making: in other words, on the assumption that integration is a political process after all. But if integration is a political process, the functionalist model is inappropriate to it; and, if the functionalist model is inappropriate, the present institutional structure—which is based on the functionalist model—is inappropriate as well. If direct elections are to benefit the Community, the contradiction between the logic implied by the decision to hold them, and the logic underlying the present Community structure, must somehow be resolved. If it is not, their most likely result will be endless confusion and conflict. The question of how to resolve it is therefore one of the most urgent in Community politics.

It is not an easy question to answer. One obvious way would be to scrap the existing structure and start again. But although that solution has some attractions on paper, they are outweighed by its practical disadvantages. With all its faults, the present structure exists and has existed for more than twenty-five years; during that time, it has displayed a remarkable capacity to adapt itself to changing circumstances. It is now quite deeply entrenched, and has a number of vested interests clustered around it. Familiarity has given it a kind of legitimacy, which a completely new structure would lack. For all these reasons, a head-on attack on it would divide the forces that support integration at a time when they badly need to hold together. In any case, it is almost always more difficult to agree on a completely new structure than on modifications to an old one, if only because a proposal to modify an old one raises fewer questions of principle and entails considering a narrower range of options. A proposal to create a completely new Community structure would waken all kinds of sleeping dogs which are much better left to their slumbers. British anti-marketeers would use it as an excuse to reopen the question of British membership. French Gaullists (and, for that matter, French Communists) would demand guarantees of the inviolability of French national sovereignty. The old, dead question of whether the Community should be 'federal' or 'confederal' would walk again. If reform had been tried and failed—or if determined attempts to achieve reform had got nowhere—there would be a strong case for trying to create a new structure, and for mobilising public opinion behind its creation. As things are, it is more sensible to try and modify the existing one.

How should this be done? Piecemeal adaptation is an attractive slogan—at least to pragmatic British ears—but it can easily become a substitute for thought. It is not enough to decide to work 'along the grain' of the existing system, to borrow a phrase from one of the best recent discussions of these matters,[8] since the existing system has a number of different grains, which run in different directions. Some grains will have to be preferred to others, and the choice will have to be based on criteria of some sort. It would be foolish to spend time trying to devise an ideal institutional structure for the Community, divorced from present realities, but it would be as foolish to rely on finding *ad hoc* solutions to the problems to which the present structure will give rise after they have made themselves felt. The contradiction described above cannot be resolved without substantial changes in the entire institutional triangle of Council-Commission-Parliament. The best way to decide what changes to make is to develop a coherent conception of the part which the elected Parliament should play in the integration process.

If this is to be done, however, another latent contradiction in the present Community structure will have to be cleared up. The constitutional model set out in the Treaty—if model is not too pompous a word—is a strange hotch-potch. It is based on the conceptions of parliamentary government and ministerial responsibility common to most West European parliamentary systems, and partly on the quite different conception of the separation of powers which is the central feature of the American Constitution, and which can also be detected in the Constitution of the present French Fifth Republic. Thus, the Commission can be dismissed by a parliamentary vote of censure, in the way that Governments in parliamentary systems can be dismissed by their Parliaments. Like Governments in Parliamentary systems, the Commission is obliged to answer written and oral parliamentary questions. Like ministers in parliamentary systems, its members attend and participate in parliamentary debates. These traces of the European conception of parliamentary government, however, co-exist uneasily with much bigger traces of the American doctrine of the separation of powers. The Commission and Parliament are separately appointed. Though Parliament can dismiss the Commission as a body, it has no say in its composition and, in any case, cannot dismiss individual Commissioners. Though Commissioners can take part in parliamentary debates, they cannot be Members of the Parliament and will not be able to be, even when the Parliament is directly elected.

Like the previous one, this contradiction has not mattered

much in the past. Though Parliament has occasionally emitted a mild growl of protest at the Commission's high-handed approach to it, and although Commissioners have sometimes grumbled peevishly to their *cabinets* about Parliament's undisciplined and unbusinesslike ways, the relationship between the two institutions has on the whole been harmonious enough. Parliament has made no serious attempt to gain power at the Commission's expense, and the Commission has seen Parliament as an ally, not as a rival. Neither side has had to think seriously about the relationship between them, and nor has anyone else. After direct elections, however, this will no longer be the case. It will become necessary for the first time to think out precisely what the relationship between the two bodies ought to be; and the latent contradiction between 'American' and 'European' elements will have to be resolved.

This means that it is necessary to decide which of the two models is appropriate for the Community. There is not much doubt about the answer. The American model has great attractions. It almost certainly provides a better basis for uniting a continent—and perhaps for governing any complex modern society—than does the European model. The fierce localism of the nineteenth-century American Congress undoubtedly helped to knit the union together, but the executive branch (greatly helped by the judiciary) played a much more important part in the process than did the legislature. It is never easy to strike the right balance between the need for strong and speedy executive action and the need for democratic scrutiny and control. More than once in American history, the balance has been wrong. But it is even more difficult to strike the right balance in a European system, where the legislature tends either to be far too assertive in the face of weak Governments, as in Fourth Republic France, or far too subservient in face of overmighty ones, as in modern Britain. Moreover, the Community system is closer to the American model than to the European; and basing its future development on the American model would raise fewer problems of adaptation.

Unfortunately, however, there is a much more powerful practical argument on the other side. One of the chief objects of the whole exercise is to correct the institutional imbalance described in the last chapter, as a result of which the institution which is supposed to provide the impetus for integration lacks the authority to do its job. The Community needs a 'motor of integration' with the force of democratic legitimacy behind it. The question, therefore, is, which model can do this better? The executive branch of the American Government has, of course, as much authority as Governments have in the parliamentary systems of Western Europe and the British Commonwealth. But its authority is derived from the fact that the President of the United States is directly elected by the people. The Community equivalent would be the direct election of the President of the Commission — and, in the foreseeable future at any rate, this is a prospect from which even the most *communautaire* member Government would certainly flinch. A directly elected Commission President would be a rival to every head of government in the Community. It has been difficult enough to persuade Member Governments to accept the direct election of an almost powerless European Parliament, even though its election is clearly laid down in the Treaty. To persuade them to accept the direct election of a Commission President who already possesses certain powers, and whose authority would be enormously augmented by being directly elected, when the election of the President is not laid down in the Treaty at all, would be an impossible task.

To try to build on the 'American' elements in the Treaty would therefore be building on sand. However unsatisfactory it may be in other respects, the European model is the only possible one for the Community. It follows that if the dangers in direct elections are to be avoided, and the opportunities seized, a deliberate decision must be made to bring the constitution of the Community into closer conformity with the West European parliamentary norm. What that entails in practice will be discussed in the next chapter.

5

A Parliamentary Europe

Community Europe is overwhelmingly a technocrats' Europe. Except during the long summer holidays, when it is practically deserted, Brussels seethes with committee meetings, at which civil servants talk to other civil servants about the policies suggested by yet more civil servants. Before framing proposals, Commission officials consult their opposite numbers from the national administrations at 'expert' working groups in Brussels, and often more informally as well. There are endless meetings within the Commission itself, at which officials from one directorate-general try to find common ground with officials from other directorates-general. Commission officials consult officials from the trade unions' and employers' organisations, and are, in turn, lobbied by them. When the Commission has finally hammered out its proposals, they are considered in yet more meetings, held under the aegis of the Council of Ministers, at which the same national and Commission officials battle formally over the points which they have previously discussed informally. Eventually, the proposals reach the summit of officialdom, the weekly meeting of C O R E P E R, from where they proceed at last to the politicians in the Council of Ministers. Like the 'outputs' of any other system of government, the policies which finally emerge from this cumbersome machinery are sometimes good and sometimes bad. But, good or bad, they are almost always tardy, and they rarely inspire much public enthusiasm.

These two facts are closely connected. Community policies emerge tardily partly because they do not inspire public enthusiasm. They do not inspire public enthusiasm partly because their gestation periods are so long. Behind that vicious circle, moreover, lies another, more damaging and more complicated one. As we have seen, one of the reasons why the pace of integration has been so slow is that the Commission — which alone has the technical and juridical authority to provide the impetus for further integration — lacks the democratic legitimacy to play its proper part in the Community system. But one of the reasons why the Commission lacks democratic legitimacy is that, although large numbers of critically important decisions are now taken by Community authorities, integration has not yet gone far enough to make the undemocratic nature of the system either obvious or intolerable. By the same token, if monetary union were established or majority voting institutionalised, the need to make Community decision-makers unambiguously answerable to the Community's electorate would be plain for all to see. But because Community decision-makers are not democratically accountable at Community level, systematic majority voting or monetary union would create a 'democratic deficit', unacceptable in a Community committed to democratic principles. Thus the Community is trapped. It fails to make progress because its system of government does not conform adequately to the norms of pluralist democracy as they are understood in its Member States. Its system remains inadequately democratic because it has not made much progress. Direct elections will not automatically spring this trap, though they will do more than any previous development in the Community's history to provide the means by which it can be sprung. The only sure way of springing it is to turn the technocratic Europe we know today into a parliamentary Europe, in which the 'accountability gap', which would in present circumstances result from either systematic majority voting or monetary union, and the 'legitimacy gap', which provides the chief explanation for the slow rate of progress of recent years, can both be closed.

This will require considerable skill, courage and resolution on the part of the directly elected Members and, indeed, on the part of all supporters of further integration. It will also require imagination and intellectual rigour. For there are conceptual obstacles to overcome as well as political ones, and in some ways the conceptual obstacles are the more formidable. It would be easy enough to devise a parliamentary constitution for a federal Europe. Australia, Canada, Federal Germany and Switzerland all provide possible models; and it would be a relatively simple exercise to decide which model was the most suitable, and what changes had to be made in it. It would not be very difficult to decide what balance between parliamentary power and governmental power is appropriate for an association of sovereign states, linked together for some common purpose, like NATO, or the O.E.C.D. But neither of these is required. The Community is a moving train, not a stationary terminus: a process, not a structure. It is not yet a federal state, and perhaps it never will be. Nor, however, is it a mere association of sovereign states. It is an association of sovereign states, which was created with the deliberate and explicit intention that it should gradually develop into something different, and which already possesses certain attributes, of great importance to its day-to-day activities, which point the way to something different. More important still, its value to its members depends on its ability to develop into something different — and to do so at a faster pace than that of the last fifteen years.

What is needed, then, is a constitution which not only permits, but actively facilitates, further evolution: a set of arrangements which suits the Community's present needs, which gives more weight than is given at present to the centripetal forces in Community politics and less to the centrifugal ones, and which can be adapted without serious difficulty to the new needs which can be expected to appear as and when those centripetal forces push the Community along the path to greater supranationality. No single set of proposals is likely to achieve all of these aims with equal ease and success. But proposals which are not even designed to achieve them all, at any rate in part, are not likely to be of much use. To adapt a phrase of the late Jimmy Maxton, Community constitution-mongers must at least aspire to ride three horses at once. Those who do not would do better to stay out of the ring.

It follows that proposals which ignore the crucial, *dynamic* aspect of the Community—proposals which are based, knowingly or otherwise, on the assumption that integration has already gone as far as it can go, or is about to go as far as it can go — are almost certain to be unsatisfactory. The same applies to proposals which overemphasise its dynamism, to proposals whose authors tacitly assume that there are no serious impediments to further integration, and imagine it is possible to devise a structure which would be appropriate in a more fully integrated Community, without paying any attention to the need to speed up the pace of integration. It also follows that analogies with national constitutional developments are almost certain to mislead. But these conclusions are much easier to state than to observe. The very fact that the Community is *sui generis* — and still more, perhaps, the fact that it is *sui generis* in a rather different way from that foreseen by its founding fathers — makes it extraordinarily difficult to understand. Though it is easy to see that national analogies are likely to be inappropriate, analogies often provide the easiest way of coming to grips with the unfamiliar, and the only analogies available are national ones. Because of all this, discussion about the Community's institutional structure often falls into one of two traps. Sometimes it is narrowly time-bound, imprisoned in the parameters of the Community as it is. At other times, it is oddly time-free, airily indifferent to the processes which will have to be understood and mastered before the Community as it is can be transformed into the Community as it ought to be. By the same token national analogies loom large, though often without being acknowledged as such, with the result that much of the discussion is conducted on a false basis.

Parliament's Legislative Powers

The relationship between the directly elected Parliament and the two other main Community institutions must be determined against this background. It is easy enough to see what needs to be done. Somehow or other the 'accountability gap' and 'legitimacy gap' described above have to be closed, and they have to be closed in a way that will make further integration easier to achieve: the famous institutional triangle has to be redrawn in such a way as to achieve these two aims. It is not so easy to do it. If the Community were already supranational, the 'legitimacy gap' would not matter and the 'accountability gap' could be closed quite easily. The European Parliament could take over the legislative powers at present exercised by the Council, so that it, rather than the Council, took the decisions on Commission proposals. The 'accountability gap' would disappear, at any rate so far as legislation is concerned, since Community laws would then be enacted by a Community legislature, responsible to the Community electorate. Much the same would be true if Parliament and Council had equal power over legislation. In that case, the Community system would be rather like the American system, in which Acts of Congress need the consent of both Houses. The Council of Ministers would be a sort of Senate and the European Parliament would be a sort of House of Representatives. But neither of these solutions is remotely practicable at the present stage of integration. They could be applied only if the Community had already become an autonomous political entity, independent of the nation states; and the reason it faces the difficulties described in this book is that it has not. None of the big Member States is yet prepared to transfer power to the Community on the scale which either of these solutions would require, and it is far from clear that many of the small Member States are prepared to do so either. Equality of legislative power between Parliament and Council should be the long-term aim, but the practical question at the present stage of integration is how to move towards it, not what to do when it is reached.

That question has been discussed a good deal in the last ten years, and a number of answers have been suggested. In 1972, the Vedel Report on *The Enlargement of Powers of the European Parliament* proposed an ingenious scheme by which Parliament's legislative powers would be increased in two stages.[1] During the first stage, Parliament was to be given powers of veto (described in the report as 'co-decision') over a limited range of subjects, and powers of delay (described as a 'suspensory veto') over a wider range. In the second stage, Parliament's suspensive powers over the latter class of subjects were to be raised to a power of co-decision. The Vedel Committee thought that, in the first stage, Parliament should be given powers of co-decision only over legislation affecting either the Community's relations with other persons in international law, or its own constitution. In practice, these include the revision of the Treaties; the admission of new members; the ratification of international agreements concluded by the Community; and the interpretation of the 'evolutive' article 235 of the Rome Treaty, which empowers the Council, acting unanimously on a proposal of the Commission, to take 'appropriate measures' to achieve one of the objectives of the Community even if the Treaty has not provided the necessary powers. The areas in which Vedel and his colleagues thought that Parliament should have delaying powers in the first stage, and powers of co-decision in the second stage, were measures harmonising national legislation and measures dealing with questions of principal arising out of the common policies which might give rise to harmonisation measures.

In a draft report for the Political Affairs Committee of the European Parliament in 1975,[2] the late Sir Peter Kirk put forward two proposals, which would have taken Parliament some way along the road to the destination set out in the Vedel Report. In the legislative field, he suggested that Parliament could be given a power of initiative, analogous to the right of a British M.P. to bring in Private Members' Bills. A Parliamentary committee would draft legislation; if the Bureau approved, the draft would be voted on in plenary session. If approved there, it would be sent to the Commission. The Commission would then submit it to the Council in the usual way. Thereafter it would follow the normal course of Community legislation. Sir Peter's second suggestion was that the so-called 'concertation procedure',[3] which already exists in the budgetary field, should be extended to all Community legislation. When the Commission had made up its mind to make a legislative proposal, it would send the text to Parliament. Parliament would then debate the Commission's proposal—before it had been set to the Council and before the Governments started to entrench their positions. The Commission would then send its proposal to the Council, together with any amendments passed by Parliament. The Council would then make a decision on the Commission's proposal, and also on Parliament's amendments; and it would do so in public, not in secret. If the Council differed at all from Parliament, the latter would hold a second debate. If, within a specified time limit, the Council refused to change its decision so as to agree with Parliament, or *vice versa*, the concertation procedure would automatically come into operation.

Taken together, these suggestions map out a path for the development of Parliament's legislative powers which at first sight seems highly attractive. At the end of the road would come complete equality of power with the Council, on the lines of the relationship between the American House of Representatives and Senate. Immediately before that would come co-decision, on the lines suggested by Vedel — in other words, the grant to Parliament of veto powers in a wide range of the most important areas of Community activity. Before that would come Vedel's 'suspensory veto'. Parliament would begin the long march to full equality through the extension of the concertation procedure from the budgetary field to the whole field of Community law making, and through the acquisition of a right of initiative complementing that of the Commission.

It is a neat scheme. But, like many neat schemes, it ignores a number of awkward problems. The most obvious, though by no means the most important, is that all but the first stage would involve significant concessions of power on the part of the Member States. Co-decision *à la Vedel* would involve amendments to the Treaty. Though Vedel and his colleagues considered that the suspensory veto would not involve such amendments, it seems unlikely that the British and French Governments, at any rate, will agree to even a suspensory veto in the near future. But it would be wrong to make too much of that. One of the tasks of the directly elected Parliament will be to fight for transfers of power from the national to the Community level. The fact that some Member Governments are likely to resist is not a reason for flinching from the battle. If the Community is to avoid slipping back, French and British attitudes will have to change; part of the purpose of discussing Community politics at all is to persuade people that they ought to change. A much more serious problem is that some of Vedel's proposals overestimated the Community's dynamism, with the result that the earlier stages on the path just sketched out do not all lead to the final destination. For the reasons already given, full legislative equality between Council and Parliament is possible only in a much more integrated Community. A prerequisite of full legislative equality is therefore more and speedier integration. But granting Parliament delaying powers over Community legislation would not speed integration up. Unless the whole exercise turned out to be a meaningless charade, it would slow it down.

It is true, of course, that any increase in Parliament's legislative powers will strengthen its capacity to delay decisions; and it would be wrong to rule out all increases on those grounds. If the price of a really big step towards closing the 'accountability gap' is an even more slow-moving legislative process, the price might well be worth paying. But Vedel's 'suspensory veto' is not a big enough step to justify such a high price. These objections do not, however, apply to his power of 'co-decision'. That too would make it easier for Parliament to delay legislation. But it would do so much to close the 'accountability gap', and it would change the whole balance of Community power so fundamentally, that the risk of further delay would be justified. If the European Parliament had a veto on legislation in a given area of Community activity, it could itself be held to account for all decisions in that area, for by definition no such decision could have been taken without its consent. The earliest possible achievement of co-decision in the areas mentioned by Vedel should therefore be an urgent priority. For rather different reasons, Sir Peter Kirk's suggestion that it should be possible to apply the concertation procedure to all Community legislation is equally unobjectionable. It would not go very far towards closing the 'accountability gap' — though Sir Peter's proposal that the Council of Ministers should be obliged to sit in public when considering Parliament's amendments to Commission proposals would make it much easier for national Parliaments to hold their Ministers to account than it is at present — but it would give Parliament a few more teeth than it has now, while creating only a small risk of further delay. His suggestion that Parliament should be given a right of initiative complementing the Commission's has even less to be said against it. It would not create any further delay to speak of, and it would add a useful, if unspectacular, new weapon to Parliament's meagre arsenal.

Parliament and the Budget

Similar considerations apply to the budgetary field, where Parliament's scanty existing powers are largely concentrated. As we have already noted, Parliament has no power over Community revenue raising. Its power over Community spending differs according to whether the spending is 'obligatory' or 'non-obligatory'. The distinction is set out in the Treaty, in which 'obligatory' spending is defined as expenditure necessarily resulting from the Treaty, or from acts adopted in accordance with the Treaty. In practice, this accounts for 75 per cent of total Community spending, including almost all agricultural spending. 'Non-obligatory expenditure' is expenditure on the administrative running costs of the Community, and on policy areas not covered by the Treaty — a category which includes, to take the most important example, expenditure on the Regional Fund. The procedure sounds complicated, but the essential principles are simple enough. First, the Commission prepares a draft budget, which is sent to the Council. The Council amends the Commission draft — voting by qualified majority — and the revised draft is then considered by Parliament. Parliament can propose modifications in the 'obligatory' sector only by an absolute majority of its total membership, but amendments in the 'non-obligatory' sectors can be passed by a simple majority of the members present. The Council then considers Parliament's amendments. Amendments in the 'obligatory' sector can be accepted only by a qualified majority; and amendments not so accepted are automatically rejected. In the 'non-obligatory' sector, however, the Council can alter Parliament's amendments only by a qualified majority. Finally, Parliament has a second reading on the Council's amendments to its amendments. In the 'obligatory' sector it can make no further changes. In the 'non-obligatory' sector, however, it can amend the Council's amendments by a majority of its total membership and a three-fifths majority of the votes cast. Last, but by no means least, Parliament has the power to reject the Budget altogether.[4]

Some of these powers are more apparent than real. Parliament's power to reject the Budget *in toto* looks at first sight like an extremely potent weapon, and enthusiastic parliamentarians could be forgiven for seeing themselves as latter-day Hampdens or Pyms, using Parliament's right to refuse supply as a lever to gain power over policy decisions. But the world has changed since the seventeenth century. Hampden and Pym did not want the King to spend more of the taxpayers' money: the European Parliament generally wants to spend more than the Council does. The right to reject the Community Budget *in toto* would be of great value if Community spending accounted for a grossly excessive proportion of Community G.D.P., or if the European Parliament consisted exclusively of dedicated advocates of expenditure cuts. In fact, the Community Budget is pathetically small, and a precondition of further supranationalism is that it should be rapidly and substantially increased. Partly for that reason, there is no pressure for Budget cuts in the European Parliament: the pressure is all the other way. In these circumstances, its right to reject the Budget looks suspiciously like a right to cut off its nose to spite its face. Parliament's powers in the 'obligatory' sector amount to a power to make a minor nuisance of itself and to force the Council to take its suggestions into account. In the 'non-obligatory' sector, however, it is a different story. There Parliament has genuine powers — powers, moreover, which can serve as the foundation for the acquisition of further power in future. It is true that there are limits on its freedom to increase expenditure in this category. Under the Treaty, the Commission has to establish a so-called 'maximum rate' — arrived at by a complicated formula, which takes account of the growth in Community G.D.P., the rate of inflation and budgetary trends in the Member States — and Parliament cannot increase even 'non-obligatory' expenditure by more than that. It is also true that parliamentary control over the Budget is in any case somewhat artificial if Parliament has no control over the policies of which the Budget is a reflection. The fact remains that it can increase expenditure, and that it can re-allocate it. The fact also remains than an adroit and determined use of these powers could give it a bigger say in making the policies which produce the expenditure.

In 1977, for example, the Commission agreed to take part in a joint committee with Parliament to co-ordinate the administration of the funds which both institutions were to spend on information programmes about direct elections. It did this not because it wanted to, but because it realised, to the dismay of the Commission officials concerned, that, if it refused, Parliament would block the budgetary appropriation enabling it to embark on the information programme. The episode was, no doubt, a trivial one, but it was an instructive one as well. It proved that a skilful operator can sometimes use negative power in a positive way; and it provided an excellent pointer to the way in which the directly elected Parliament — given the right combination of guile and awkwardness — could insert itself into the decision-making process in more important fields.

How, then, should Parliament's budgetary role evolve? Abolition of the distinction between 'obligatory' and 'non-obligatory' expenditure would clearly give it substantially more power than it has at present. The funds devoted to agricultural intervention buying, for example, would then be controlled by Parliament, and as a result Parliament would have a decisive voice in the development of the common agricultural policy. Like legislative equality between Council and Parliament, however, this presupposes a much more supranational Community than has so far been achieved. The distinction between 'obligatory' and 'non-obligatory' expenditure, and between Parliament's puny role in the former and its weighty role in the latter, reflects the present balance between the Community as a treaty-bound association of sovereign states, and the Community as a developing political entity in its own right. Majority voting in the Council of Ministers on budgetary matters, Parliament's role in the 'non-obligatory' sector, indeed the very concept of 'non-obligatory' expenditure itself, all reflect the Community's status as a developing entity, capable of putting unanticipated flesh on to the bones laid out in the Treaty. Council control over the 'obligatory' sector, and through that over the Community's one really important piece of positive integration, reflects its status as an association of sovereign states.[5] The distinction will have to be abolished sooner or later, and supporters of a more supranational community should press for its abolition. But they should recognise that abolition is unlikely to come quickly. As with legislative equality between Council and Parliament, the question that matters for the present and immediate future is how Parliament's budgetary powers can be increased in other ways.

The answer is threefold. Expenditure control is not only a matter of deciding big categories of expenditure year by year. It is also a matter of ensuring that money voted to particular purposes is spent on the purposes for which it was voted, and of scrutinising the forward projections of expenditure to see how far they fit the policy priorities of the spending authority, and how far those priorities fit the real needs of the taxpayers whose money is being spent. In all this, the European Parliament is still sadly deficient. As we have seen, the Budget Committee now has a control sub-committee, which performs some of the 'post hoc' functions of the British Public Accounts Committee. A Court of Auditors has also been set up as a safeguard against fraud. But parliamentary control over expenditure which has already been carried out is of far less political significance than parliamentary control over the forward planning of expenditure. What matters politically is to ensure that policies are adapted to the purposes they are supposed to serve, and that spending programmes are adapted to the policies which gave rise to them. As the Procedure Committee of the British House of Commons showed ten years ago, this is difficult enough even in a single Member State, with a highly developed parliamentary tradition, one of the central elements in which is the notion that one of Parliament's main functions is to control Government spending.[6] Vested interests cluster around all spending programmes, and almost by definition they act as a barrier against change. Chief among these vested interests, moreover, are the bureaucracies which operate the programmes. Policy makers are therefore under enormous pressure to continue the existing pattern of public spending, for no better reason than that it is the existing pattern.

If this is true of a single nation state, it is far more true of the Community, where bureaucracies proliferate, where political control is minimal and where there is therefore an even greater danger that the pattern of public spending will be determined by administrative inertia and departmental log-rolling rather than by any rational assessment of needs and priorities. Even more than the nation states which make it up, the Community lacks clear criteria on which to base its decisions about where to intervene and where not to do so. As the MacDougall Group pointed out, the only sensible criterion is one based on the concept of economies of scale.[7] The Community should perform those functions which it can perform more efficiently than Member Governments can, but it should refrain from acquiring functions which Member Governments can perform more efficiently. The criterion is far from being observed at present. Not only do Member Governments obstinately insist on performing functions which could be better performed by the Community, but eager Commission officials are constantly trying to acquire functions for the Community which can be performed much better by Member Governments. Often the motives of those concerned are praiseworthy and the policies they put forward, admirable. But that is not the point. The point is that the Commission is wasting its time and the taxpayers' money if it puts forward even admirable policies in areas in which the Community ought not to be involved at all. One of the most useful, and most politically rewarding, ways in which the directly elected Parliament could cut its teeth would be to carry out a systematic appraisal of the cost-effectiveness of the whole range of Community policies, judged by the MacDougall criterion.

To do that it will need new machinery of its own and a change of practice on the part of the Commission. Here too the Kirk Report provides the best guide to what is necessary. At present, when the Commission puts forward a new proposal for an act with financial implications, the Budget Committee gives its opinion to the Committee which has to deal with the substance of the proposal. It takes two factors into account — its view of the substantive merits of the proposal, and its view of whether or not the proposal is sensible in budgetary terms. Its task is then fulfilled. Sir Peter believed that Parliament did not have an adequate opportunity for detailed scrutiny of the expenditure involved in the Commission proposals, or a genuine voice in assessing the policy options open to the Commission. Accordingly, he recommended that the Commission should be asked to submit to Parliament a detailed financial schedule with each proposal for an act with financial implications. This would make it possible to introduce a two-pronged, 'before and after', control system over Community expenditure. Each Parliamentary Committee would set up a budgetary sub-committee, which would be expected to examine all the relevant financial information concerning, not only individual proposals for acts with financial implications, but the total budget for the work of the Directorates-General concerned. This would enable the parent committees to assess all the significant policy options open to the Commission in that sector. Wherever appropriate, the sub-committees were to operate through public hearings — cross-examining Commissioners and members of their staffs, and seeking evidence from independent experts.[8] Machinery of this kind would give the European Parliament far sharper budgetary teeth than it possesses today, without encroaching in any way on the prerogatives of the Council of Ministers, without necessitating the slightest change in the Treaties and without incurring the wrath of anti-integrationist politicians in Britain and France. Yet if the teeth were used properly, Parliament's real influence on Community policy-making would be enormously increased.

The second way in which Parliament should try to increase its budgetary powers is more controversial. At present, it has the last word on a quarter of total Community spending, but no power at all over Community revenue-raising. This is clearly an anomaly, and in principle an objectionable anomaly. It means that Parliament — the only body through which Community decision-making can be made politically responsible — is itself not fully responsible to the public. If the power to spend is divorced from the power to tax, the public have no opportunity to balance the spenders' boons against the taxers' imposts, and the spenders can escape the consequences of their decisions. As the MacDougall Group have pointed out, the revenues available to the Community are approaching their limit, and there is growing concern over their regressive nature.

In these circumstances, a determined parliamentary effort to acquire taxing powers might win widespread support. If it acquired such powers, the imposition of a 'maximum rate' beyond which it cannot increase expenditure in the 'non-obligatory' sector — which can be justified at present on the grounds that it prevents irresponsible spending decisions — would no longer be necessary.

Parliament and Monetary Union

Parliament's third route to greater budgetary power is through monetary union — or, rather, through the budgetary decisions which are a precondition of monetary union. As we have seen, monetary union would be intolerable to the weaker Member States without a Community budget at least ten times as large as the present one, while effective movement towards monetary union would require a Community budget around two-and-a-half times as big as the present one. The additional expenditure thus created would nearly all be 'non-obligatory'. Thus, moves towards monetary union, accompanied by the kind of fiscal redistribution without which monetary union is out of the question, would lead *ipso facto* to a substantial increase in Parliament's budgetary powers. The MacDougall Group suggested that the increased expenditure which they advocated for the stage before full monetary union should be concentrated in the three areas of regional policy, labour-market policy and unemployment compensation. At present Community spending in the first two is around one-twentieth of the expenditure carried out by Member Governments, while in the third there is no Community spending at all. The MacDougall Group suggested that the Community's spending should be raised to around a third of Member-State expenditure in all three.[9] If this were done, the European Parliament would acquire, through its powers over 'non-obligatory' expenditure, a really significant say in three of the most politically sensitive policy areas in modern Europe. So far as monetary union is concerned, therefore, an important part of the 'democratic deficit' described earlier in this book is self-cancelling. Monetary union requires extra expenditure: extra expenditure, at any rate in the fields in which it would have to come if monetary union were to be established, automatically increases Parliament's powers.

This applies only to part of the deficit, however, not to all of it. At present, national Governments are accountable to their Parliaments, and through them to their electorates, for monetary and exchange-rate policy. It is true that central banks usually manage these matters, and that Parliaments rarely have much control over the day-to-day activities of the banks. But that does not detract from their ability to hold their Governments to account, and still less from the electorate's ability to do so. Messrs Callaghan and Healey cannot escape responsibility for the level of interest rates or the parity of the pound by explaining that it is the Bank of England and not the Government which decides such things. If they tried to do so they would rightly be disbelieved. In a monetary union, this would no longer be true. Monetary and exchange-rate policy would not be decided by national authorities, and national prime ministers and finance ministers could no longer be held to account for them. It would be as absurd to blame the British Chancellor of the Exchequer for the rate of interest in the United Kingdom as to blame the chairman of the Greater Manchester finance committee for the rate of interest in Manchester. But although decisions about the money supply and the exchange rate would no longer be taken by national authorities, they would have to be taken by someone. The notion that that someone could be an unelected committee of Platonic guardians, accountable only to their own consciences, is clearly a fantasy, and a rather unattractive fantasy at that. It would certainly break down in practice, since decisions taken by an unelected body of guardians would have no legitimacy, and could not be made to stick against determined pressure from elected Governments. It is also wrong in principle, since decisions about the money supply and the exchange rate are among the most important taken in any modern economy, and in a democracy those who take important decisions must be accountable to the people or to the elected representatives of the people. Unless monetary union is to violate some of the most central of the democratic values for which the Community claims to stand, the body or bodies which will have to be set up to manage it must be made accountable to the European Parliament.

This was clearly understood in an earlier stage of the debate on monetary union. The Werner Report was firmly committed to the principle of parliamentary accountability. It envisaged the creation of two Community bodies — a 'centre of decision' for economic policy and a Community system for the central banks. The former was to have been entrusted with the formation of Community economic policy, and was to have been directly responsible to the European Parliament.[10] In more recent stages of the debate, however, little thought has been given to the institutional implications in general, and less to the crucial parliamentary ones in particular. A paper by Professor O'Donoghue in Volume II of the MacDougall Report yields the not uninteresting insight that, if the European Parliament's budgetary powers were to be increased, Parliament might throw up an embryonic Executive from the prevailing majority, by which the decisions would actually be taken.[11] For all practical purposes, the rest is silence. The pros and cons of monetary union have been discussed almost wholly in economic terms. Virtually nothing has been said — by either supporters or opponents — about the need to ensure that the powers which national Parliaments would have to lose are subjected to parliamentary control at the Community level. More ominously still, the architects of the E.M.S. — which is either a move towards monetary union or an exercise in monetary wishful thinking — appear to have been oblivious to these considerations. Even the Commission, whose decision to re-open the debate on monetary union in 1977 helped to pave the way for Chancellor Schmidt's initiative in 1978, has said hardly anything about them, apart from an interesting aside, in a parliamentary speech by its President, to the effect that the American Federal Reserve Board is ultimately answerable to the United States Congress.[12]

If the directly elected Parliament is to be taken seriously, one of its first priorities must be to put this situation right. It will have to fight for a parliamentary voice in the evolution of the E.M.S., and for parliamentary scrutiny of the management of the E.M.S. More important still, it will have to fight for the principle that a prerequisite of full monetary union is parliamentary accountability and control. There are a number of ways in which parliamentary accountability might be achieved. A new 'centre of decision', to use the Werner terminology, might be specially created, with new machinery to ensure that it was answerable to Parliament. The 'centre of decision' might be the Commission, in which case it would be necessary to make Parliament's control over the Commission more of a reality. Conceivably, the 'centre of decision' might be the embryo parliamentary executive envisaged in Professor O'Donoghue's paper. But at this stage it is unnecessary — and perhaps undesirable — to discuss these questions in great detail. What is necessary is to establish the fundamental principle that the monetary authority must be responsible to the European Parliament, and that if there is a separate economic centre of decision apart from the Commission, that separate centre should be responsible to the European Parliament as well.

The 'Legitimacy Gap'

Increases in Parliament's legislative and budgetary powers on the lines sketched out above would go some way towards closing the 'accountability gap'. Except incidentally, however, they will do nothing to close the 'legitimacy gap'; and it is the 'legitimacy gap', not the 'accountability gap' which has slowed down the pace of integration. To concentrate exclusively on closing the 'accountability gap', as discussion of Parliament's place in the institutional triangle is generally apt to do, is therefore to put the cart before the horse. The most urgent task is not to see that Parliament has an appropriate place in the supranational Community which does not yet exist. It is to find a way of harnessing Parliament's new weight and authority to the needs of integration, so as to make it more likely that that supranational Community is brought into being.

In practice, this hinges on the relationship between Parliament and the Commission. As we saw in chapter 4, the American model of the separation of powers is not practicable in the Community. If the 'legitimacy gap' is to be closed, the changes needed to close it will have to conform to the European model of Parliamentary government. In pure theory, no doubt, it could be closed if Parliament itself were to take over the Commission's role as the 'motor of integration', leaving the Commission to become merely a rather bloated adjunct to the secretariat of the Council of Ministers. But this is easier said than done. Parliaments are good at reacting, but they do not find it easy to initiate. They can scrutinise and control the activities of an Executive, but they are too diffuse, too heterogeneous and too fissiparous to assume the functions of an Executive and make policy themselves. In fact Parliaments do not themselves make policy in parliamentary systems. Four elements in the parliamentary model are of particular importance in the Community context. In the first place, it is the Government, not Parliament, which makes policy. Secondly, however, the Government is responsible to Parliament and derives its authority from the fact that it needs the confidence of Parliament. Thirdly, its legislation has to be passed by Parliament and its policies have to be approved by Parliament; it is this that makes them legitimate. Fourthly, the members of the Government and a majority of the members of the Parliament belong, by definition, to the same party or group of parties, and are held together by common political loyalties. To close the 'legitimacy gap' we need Community equivalents for these.

The first two could be achieved in one of two ways. The European Parliament could throw up an Executive from within its own ranks. Alternatively, the existing embryo Executive of the Community — in other words, the Commission — could be made fully responsible to the European Parliament. The first possibility should not be dismissed out of hand. As we have seen, the Commission is cumbersome, slow-moving, and lacking in political flair. Years of searching for the lowest common denominator of agreement in the Council of Ministers and repeated buffetings from member Governments have all but destroyed the vitality and *élan* which characterised it in the early days. It has become a cautious, timid and defensive body, more anxious to cling to the slender powers which it has managed to acquire over the last twenty years than to create opinion or to change the context within which policies are made. After direct elections, at any rate, Parliament can hardly fail to be more sensitive politically, and it is likely to be more adventurous as well. In its Bureau, it already possesses an embryo Executive, and in its permanent staff an embryo civil service. Given time, the Bureau — or perhaps a committee composed of the leading figures in an alliance of party groups commanding a majority in the Assembly — might well evolve into a sort of European Cabinet. As Professor O'Donoghue pointed out, the further development of Parliament's budgetary powers, which will become inevitable if the Budget is increased along Mac-Dougall lines, will in any event generate pressures pushing Parliament along this road.

But although it would be wrong to rule out such a development *a priori*, it would entail considerable short and medium-term disadvantages. The most obvious is that, unless the Treaty were amended, the Commission would still retain its existing monopoly of the right of initiative. Unless it were to acquiesce in Parliament's effectively replacing it — and on past form, at any rate, this seems so unlikely as to be virtually inconceivable — there would be endless jurisdictional conflicts between the two institutions. At least in the early stages of such a development, moreover, Parliamentary initiatives, in most cases presumably passed by only a majority, might have less force than Commission initiatives have. For all these reasons it would be better for the Commission to remain as the Community's policy-initiating and executive body, with Parliament supplying the legitimacy which the Commission now lacks.

Parliament and the Commission

In that case, however, the Commission will have to be made responsible to the European Parliament in a much fuller sense than it is at present. It cannot be made completely responsible without amending the Treaty; given current French and British attitudes, it must be assumed that amendments to the Treaty designed, as these would be, to increase the Commission's authority, are unlikely in the near future. The Commission has, however, a perfect right to propose amendments to the Treaties, and it should prepare proposals for full responsibility — notably by giving Parliament a voice in the appointment of the Commission, and particularly of its President — and submit them to Parliament and then to the Council, as soon as possible. Even without Treaty amendment, moreover, it could take some steps along the road to full responsibility. Three are particularly desirable. In the first place, it should voluntarily submit itself to a vote of confidence immediately after the directly elected Parliament assembles. Thereafter, it should agree to treat a vote of no confidence, passed by simple majority of the Parliament, as equivalent to a vote of censure necessitating its resignation, even if the motion does not get the two-thirds majority stipulated by the Treaty. Thirdly, it should decide that an individual Commissioner who loses Parliament's confidence must resign, even if the Commission as a whole retains it.

The first of these suggestions is self-explanatory. The Commission would clearly gain moral and political authority if the new Parliament's first act was to pass a vote of confidence in it; while if it turned out to be unable to win Parliament's confidence then, its chances of doing so later would clearly be very small. It would be nothing more than a gesture, however, though a gesture of great symbolic value.

The second and third proposals are more complicated, and raise more difficulties. At present, Parliament can dismiss the Commission by passing a censure motion by a two-thirds majority of its total membership. That power has sometimes been referred to as a 'nuclear weapon', so deadly that it can never be used; and, so far, no censure motion has, in fact, been passed. It is nevertheless of enormous symbolic and constitutional importance. It is the one really deadly sanction which Parliament possesses over the Commission. Much more important, it is the source of such democratic legitimacy as the Commission possesses. If Parliament had no such power over the Commission, the Commission would be solely the creature of the Member Governments by whom it is appointed. It is only because it can be deprived of office by Parliament, that it can claim to have Parliament's confidence; and it is only because it can claim to have Parliament's confidence that it can claim to be in part a political, and not a purely bureaucratic, body.

A Commission freed of parliamentary control would be a Commission with no political base whatever; one of the reasons why its political base is at present too slender for it to play its proper role is that Parliament's control over it is too tenuous. But the more difficult it is for Parliament to censure the Commission, the more tenuous is its control over the Commission, and the weaker therefore is the Commission's claim to have Parliament's confidence. To lower the requirement for passing a censure motion from a two-thirds majority of the total membership to an absolute majority would thus strengthen the Commission's legitimacy as well as Parliament's powers; and although a change in the Treaty rules would require an amendment, the object of such a change could be achieved by a unilateral Commission declaration that it intended henceforth to behave as though the amendment had been made. Like national Governments, moreover, the Commission could deliberately seek a vote of confidence from Parliament, putting its own existence at stake in doing so, in order to win extra authority for some particularly controversial proposal.

The suggestion that individual Commissioners who lose Parliament's confidence should resign, even if the Commission as a whole does not do so, has fewer advantages for the Commission, but more for Parliament. One reason why the censure motion is a 'nuclear deterrent', which no one has yet been foolhardy enough to use, is that it is manifestly unreasonable to dismiss the entire college, most of whose members may be thoroughly acceptable to Parliament, merely because the policies or actions of one member of it are unacceptable. But because Parliament has no way of punishing individual Commissioners — in the way that the British House of Commons, for example, can move to reduce the salary of an individual Minister — its control over the policies of individual Commissioners and individual Directorates-General is much less complete than it would otherwise be. Weak and incompetent Commissioners shelter behind their stronger and more competent colleagues, with damaging results for the efficiency and reputation of the Commission as a whole. It is true, of course, that if individual Commissioners could be dismissed by parliamentary vote, the Commission's 'collegiality' — by which all

Commissioners accept collective responsibility for Commission policies — might be eroded. It is also true that a party or coalition of parties with a majority in Parliament might try to force through a change in the party complexion of the Commission by getting rid of Commissioners from opposing parties. But both developments would be thoroughly healthy. The Commission's collegiality is a myth, and nothing would be lost by abandoning it. And if Parliament started to get rid of Commissioners whose politics were unacceptable to it, it would be taking an important step along the road to full responsibility.

Changes in Commission-Parliament relations are also needed in the legislative field. As we have seen, Parliament is at present consulted about Commission proposals only after they have been sent to the Council of Ministers. Partly because the Commission services usually keep in close touch with the parliamentary committees in their fields, all but a small minority of Commission proposals are in fact acceptable to Parliament, even though they have not been submitted to it before being made. If there is any disagreement, moreover, the Commission nearly always modifies its proposal to bring it into line with Parliament's Opinion.[13] The fact remains, however, that Parliament is not consulted until after the Commission has decided what proposals to make, until after it has consulted Member Governments and outside interest groups, and until after its proposals have been sent to the Council.

Here, too, a change in the legal position would require amendments to the Treaty, but here, too, the Commission could make important changes in practice on its own initiative. If it decided to send no important proposal to the Council until the substance of the proposal had been submitted to and approved by Parliament — in other words, to share its right of initiative with Parliament — it would transform the relationship between the two institutions and the realities of Community law-making without affecting the letter of the Treaty in any way. The 'legitimacy gap' would not be closed altogether, but it would be far smaller than it is today. All Commission proposals to the Council would, *ipso facto*, have the backing of the directly elected Parliament. If the Council ignored or rejected them, it would be slapping the directly elected Parliament in the face — and in a sense, therefore, the Community electorate represented in the directly elected Parliament — as well as the Commission. On paper, the existing institutional triangle would be unaffected. In reality, Commission and Parliament would both strengthen their positions a great deal, and with them the chance of moving the Community out of its present *impasse*.

These changes would greatly increase the Commission's authority, but in the short run, at any rate, they would also reduce its apparent power and freedom of action. Busy Commissioners and Commission officials would have to pay more attention to parliamentary opinion than they do now, without having to pay less to the opinions of national Governments and national administrations. Commission proposals would have a new hurdle to jump over, without ceasing to have to jump over the existing ones. The Commission could be accused of flouting the spirit of the Treaty, of which it is supposed to be the guardian; and it would have surrendered its monopoly of the right of initiative, to which it has hitherto clung with the mournful tenacity of a shipwrecked sailor clinging to a leaky raft. Much more importantly, moreover, it would also have had to make a fundamental change in its view of Parliament, and of itself. Commission and Parliament are, of course, allies already. But, in the Commission's eyes at any rate, it is very much the senior ally, and Parliament very much the junior. The changes advocated here would turn the alliance into one of equals. Indeed, in an important sense, it would no longer be an alliance at all. The Commission would have to stop seeing the Parliament as a separate institution with which it had relations. Instead it would have to see it, in Maoist language, as the water in which Commissioners had to swim.

6

A Party Europe?

So far, we have discussed the role of the European Parliament, and its future relationship with the Council and the Commission as though it were a solid, homogeneous piece of constitutional machinery, linked in various ways with other, equally homogeneous pieces of constitutional machinery. In reality, of course, it consists of almost 200 party politicians, with different ideologies, different values and different allegiances, who are in politics to further those ideologies. The Council of Ministers consists, even more obviously, of party men, whose positions depend on the support of their parties and on their capacity to further the interests of their parties. The Commission is supposed to be independent of national ties, including party ties, but most Commissioners, too, have party pasts and hopes for party futures.

Yet most discussion about the Community, and particularly about its institutional structure, is based on the tacit assumption that its development and policies can be understood without reference to party; and although that assumption has never been entirely accurate, it has contained an important element of truth. It would be impossible to write the history of the Community in the 1960s without paying at least some attention to the influence of Gaullist ideology on French policy-making, or the history of the Community since 1973 without paying similar attention to the ideological divisions within the British Labour Party. But although the Community's development has been shaped, in part, by party pressures, these pressures have made themselves felt almost wholly at the national level. The policies pursued by Member Governments in the Council of Ministers are influenced by national parties, not by Community ones, or even by Community associations of national ones. The Socialist parties of the Community are linked together in the Confederation of Socialist Parties, but the Confederation does not influence the behaviour of Socialist Governments in the Council. The fact that Helmut Schmidt and James Callaghan both wear Socialist labels may conceivably have some bearing on their relations with each other, but it has no discernible bearing on their policies towards the Community. The most important single feature of Community politics at present is the so-called axis between Bonn and Paris. The Bonn-Paris axis owes nothing whatever to party. It is hard to believe that it would be any stronger if the Christian Democrats were to replace the present Social Democratic Government in Germany. It would almost certainly be a great deal weaker if a Socialist Government were to come to power in France.

Nor is there much evidence of Community party influence on the Commission. Like the British Cabinet, the Commission operates a form of collective responsibility. In public, it pretends that all Commissioners are equally responsible for all Commission decisions, and that they all agree with all their colleagues about their decisions. At a rather deeper level, its members share a less well-formulated attitude, more difficult to summarise in a few words, which dates from the Monnet era and which probably has even more influence on their actions. The Commission sees itself as a political body, but not as a party-political body. If it is partisan, it likes to think, it is partisan only for Europe: [1] party, it feels instinctively, is at best irrelevant to the construction of Europe, and at worst positively detrimental to it. Its self-image is reinforced by its behaviour. The positions which Commissioners adopt in the Commission inevitably reflect their domestic party allegiances. But they do not form cross-national party allegiances. Six members of the present Commission are Socialists — almost a majority. But there is no discernible Socialist *bloc* in the Commission or, for that matter, any discernible anti-Socialist *bloc*. On the issues the Commission discusses week by week, opinions cut across party lines.

Until now, the same has been true of the European Parliament. To be sure, it is divided, like all self-respecting Parlia-

ments, into party groups. Members sit in the hemicycle according to their groups, not to their nationalities. The groups have
large Secretariats, go into caucus again and again during
sessions, meet frequently out of session as well and divide up
the committee chairmanships and rapporteurships between
each other. The President of the Parliament is elected in a
party vote; the proceedings of the 'Enlarged Bureau', which
decides both the sessional agenda and broad issues of institutional policy, are dominated by the group Presidents.

But all this is only the tip of a much more complicated ice-
berg. Only three of the six groups are genuinely trans-national
(see the Appendix). The Communist and Allies Group consists
of the representatives of the French and Italian Communist
parties — which are, of course, deeply divided on European
issues as well as on a whole range of other matters — and a
stray Dane. The Conservative Group consists of British Conservatives, a Danish Conservative and a member of the Danish
Centre Democratic party — a breakaway from the Danish
Social Democratic Party, which occupies a position in Danish
politics somewhat to the left of the British Liberals. The
Gaullist, or 'European Progressive Democrat', group consists
of the French Gaullists, linked in implausible wedlock with the
Irish Fianna Fail — two parties which have in common only
their support for the Common Agricultural Policy and the fact
that their doctrines, policies and emotional attitudes can be
understood only by reference to the least accessible tribal myths
of the two countries concerned. It also contains a member of
the Danish Progress (or 'anti-tax') party. The three trans-
national groups — the Socialists, the Christian Democrats and
the Liberals — are all deeply divided in doctrine and attitude.

Perhaps because of all this, the European Parliament has
seen itself until now less as a cockpit in which rival parties
fight for power than as a non-partisan pressure group for the
European ideal. Most of its influential and long-serving members have been 'good Europeans' first and party politicians
second. On the whole, they have been reluctant to bring party
conflicts into the chamber. Parliamentary debates are generally
conducted in an atmosphere of somnolent goodwill, more
reminiscent of a Church Assembly than of a Parliament in a

national capital. Though votes are taken, they are not taken very often. The norm, as one recent authority puts it, is 'the near-unanimous compromise resolution'.[2] When votes do occur, party discipline is lax. Members from the same group are slightly more prone to vote together than Members from the same country, but only slightly.[3] Like Parliament's own role in the decision-making process, the role of party in the European Parliament is decorative rather than functional. The party groups exist because Members would feel unhappy without them: because they know that proper Parliaments have parties, and because they want to prove to themselves and to others that the European Parliament is a proper Parliament. They do not exist because like-minded Members from different parts of the Community have found it necessary to band together to further causes or defend interests at the Community level. Parliament would look different if the groups ceased to exist, but it is doubtful if it would behave differently.

No national Parliament, however, could possibly be understood without reference to party. National Parliaments can also be seen as pieces of constitutional machinery, linked in various ways with other pieces of constitutional machinery. But that is not how most Members or voters in fact see them. Whatever else national Parliaments may or may not do, they are first and foremost places where political parties fight for power. Voters vote for political parties, and Members are elected as representatives of political parties. The machinery works as the parties want it to work. And the most important single feature of the 'parliamentary model' discussed in the last chapter is, of course, the fourth — the existence of strong party-political links between the Executive and a majority of members of the legislature. Parliamentary government is, in reality, party government; almost certainly, it works only because it is party government. It is only because Governments can call on the party loyalties of a majority of the legislature that they can govern with even a semblance of consistency or adopt even a semblance of a long view. If there were no party ties between Government and legislature, Governments would have to cobble together new majorities *ad hoc* for each separate item of Government policy, and consistency would be even

harder to achieve than it is already. By the same token, legisla-
tors would be under even stronger pressure to vote down
necessary, but unpopular, policies, and the time-scale of policy-
making would be even more truncated. At a different level,
moreover, the parties are the instruments through which
decision-makers can be held to account before the people for
decisions taken in the people's name. In a system like that of
the United States or Fifth Republic France, where the head
of the executive is himself subject to direct popular re-election,
accountability can be achieved without a coherent party
system. But in the European model of parliamentary government, voters can punish or reward Governments only through
the votes they cast for political parties, and the weaker and
less coherent the party system, the smaller are the electorate's
chances of holding its Government to account.

One of the main arguments of this book is that a central
weakness in the Community system is that no one can be held
unambiguously to account for decisions taken at the Community level, and one of the main purposes of the changes
discussed in the last chapter is to remedy that weakness. A precondition of accountability is a proper channel between electorate and decision-makers, so that the electorate can make its
wishes felt. In all systems based on the parliamentary model,
that channel is provided by the political parties; and although
no one would pretend that they do this perfectly, no one can
deny that if they did not exist it would not be done at all. It
follows that if the Community system of government is to be
based, however distantly, on the parliamentary model, a Community party system will be needed too. The point of trying to
close the 'accountability gap' discussed in the last chapter is not
to make the European Parliament more powerful. It is to make
the people of Europe more powerful. If that is to be done, it is as
essential to make sure that Members of the European Parliament are accountable to the electorate as to make sure that
Community decision-makers are accountable to Parliament.
A prerequisite of a people's Europe is a parliamentary Europe:
a prerequisite of a parliamentary Europe is a party Europe.

Two questions therefore arise. Is a Community party system
possible? If so, what form is it likely to take?

Direct Elections and the Parties

Clearly, no Community party system exists as yet, except perhaps in embryo. To be sure, this year's elections will be contested by three trans-national federations of parties, corresponding to the three trans-national groups in the European Parliament. The Confederation of Socialist Parties, the Federation of Liberal and Democratic Parties and the European People's Party, which links together the Community's Christian Democratic parties, have all started to frame joint manifestos, to be presented to the electorate in all the Community countries where the member parties of the federation operate. In some countries, there is likely to be a certain amount of trans-national activity. At the same time, there are signs that the national parties will be fighting the elections more fiercely than they foresaw when the decision to hold the elections was made. The elections will almost certainly have important psychological repercussions on domestic politics. Parties which do badly will be assumed to have lost the electorate's confidence; parties which do well will be assumed to have won it. Governments will be forced to do all they can to prove that they are still supported by their electorates; opposition parties will be forced to do all they can to prove that they are the favourites to win the next domestic election. In Germany, the Christian Democrats will have a splendid opportunity to undermine the Government's authority. In France, the Socialists will have an opportunity to revenge themselves, both on the Government and on the Communists, for their humiliation in the 1978 National Assembly elections.

Not only will this be true of the European elections this year. Almost certainly, it will be true of the European elections five years hence. In all the Member States of the Community, the Government's authority — and therefore its ability to govern — fluctuates with the fluctuations in its opinion-poll ratings and with the fates of its party supporters in parliamentary by-elections and in local and regional elections. The 1966 Wilson Government had a majority of almost 100 in the House of

Commons. Even so, its credibility and authority were almost destroyed by its opinion-poll and by-election reverses after devaluation in 1967. The authority and self-confidence of the Giscardien régime in France were far smaller during the long run-up to the 1978 National Assembly elections, when the opinion polls consistently put the Union of the Left ahead, than they have been since the elections, when the Government did far better than anyone had predicted. Land elections in Germany and regional elections in Italy have had similar consequences for the authority of the Governments in those two countries. Even in the least European-minded of the Member States, the European elections will be much bigger and more dramatic events than local or provincial elections, and the domestic political repercussions of success or failure in them will be correspondingly greater. The long-term effect of all this on the relations between the directly elected European Members and their parties at home — and, for that matter, on the relations between the national parties and the party groups in the European Parliament on the one hand and the trans-national federations of parties on the other — is a question for speculation. What is almost certain is that the Members will have been returned after fierce partisan campaigns, fought for high party stakes, and that their re-election will depend on the outcomes of equally fierce partisan campaigns when the life of the Parliament comes to an end. They can hardly fail to arrive in a much more partisan mood than has characterised Members of the European Parliament in the past, and they will be under strong pressure to behave in a much more partisan fashion thereafter.

Some Commissioners, at any rate, will be subject to the same pressures. Many are party politicians by origin, and expect to return to party politics when their terms of office are over. Their party colleagues at home are likely to ask awkward questions if they stand ostentatiously aloof from the party battles which direct elections will provoke. If Commissioner Giolitti is to remain on good terms with his Socialist comrades in Italy, he will have to support Socialist candidates in the elections there. If Commissioner Brunner is to achieve a future in German Liberal politics, he will have to campaign for Liberal candidates.

If Commissioner Burke is to row his way back to a berth in Irish politics, he would be well advised to appear on the hustings in support of the Irish branch of Christian Democracy. With most Commissioners, moreover, the pressures of self-interest will in any case be buttressed by the pressures of loyalty and commitment. After the elections, they are also likely to be buttressed by pressures from Parliament. The more partisan Parliament becomes, the more likely it is that Commission proposals — and the individual performances of Commission members — will be judged according to party criteria; and the more necessary it will be for Commissioners to find allies in the party groups which are closest to them. If they are to do this, they will have to adopt a more partisan approach themselves, at any rate in public. Little by little, the fiction of 'collegiality' is likely to be eroded, and the Commission is likely to become in form what it already is in fact — a coalition of party politicians, agreeing on some issues but disagreeing openly and publicly on others.

Yet it does not follow that the embryo Community system represented by the trans-national groups in the Parliament and the trans-national federations of parties which will be contesting the European elections is bound to develop into a viable organism. The trans-national federations will play parts in the election, but the national parties will play much bigger ones. For the reasons just given, the elections are likely to be fought quite fiercely, and on clearly partisan lines. But the battles will be national, not trans-national. Members of the European Parliament are likely to arrive in a strongly partisan mood, but it will be a mood of national, not Community, partisanship. The same, of course, applies to the partisan pressures to which they — and, through them, the Commission — will be subject when the elections are over. The fact that the European elections will have been fought for high domestic stakes, and that the next European elections are likely to be fought for high domestic stakes as well, will make the national parties more anxious to keep their representatives at Strasbourg and Luxembourg under control, not less. Direct elections will help to make ordinary citizens aware of what decisions are taken at Community level, and they may also make ordinary citizens more anxious than they have been in the past to make sure that these decisions accord with their wishes. At the same time, they may make national parties more conscious of their sister parties elsewhere in the Community. It does not follow that they will blur the differences between national parties which happen, often for reasons which have no contemporary relevance, to wear the same label.

National Parties and Community Issues

These differences are very marked. The German Christian Democratic party is a right-wing party, similar in outlook and attitude to the British Conservative party or to most of the American Republican party. The Italian Christian Democratic party is a vast political umbrella, covering a multitude of tendencies, which range from what in Britain would be regarded as the far right of the political spectrum to what in Britain would be regarded as the moderate left. The Belgian Social Christians would repudiate the suggestion that theirs is a conservative party in the British mould. The most prominent Belgian member of the Christian Democratic group in the European Parliament is a former miner, whose political attitudes are closer to those of the right-wing of the British Labour party than to those of the German Christian Democratic party. The differences within the Liberal family of parties are even greater. The British Liberal Party is, for most practical purposes, a social democratic party, somewhat to the left of the German S.P.D., and it would fit without much difficulty in the Socialist group in the European Parliament, alongside the French Left Radicals. The Dutch, Danish and Italian Liberals are on the right. The German Free Democrats occupy the centre of the German spectrum, which puts them on the right of the Community spectrum. The French Republicans, who count as members of the Liberal group in the European Parliament, are probably closer in ideology to the moderate, pro-European wing of the British Conservative party than to any other political grouping in the Community.

On the surface, the Socialist group is more homogeneous. Though their ancestries differ, the Socialist parties of the Community all share common memories and, to some extent at least, a common myth. All see themselves, however dimly, as the champions of the 'have nots' against the 'haves'; all pay at least intermittent lip-service to the old slogans of proletarian internationalism. Even today, it is not altogether without importance that Keir Hardie was a pall-bearer at August Bebel's funeral or that Eduard Bernstein was strongly influenced by the British Fabians. Though there are big differences between them, James Callaghan, Helmut Schmidt and François Mitterrand belong recognisably to the same political family, in a sense which is not true of Mrs Thatcher, Helmut Kohl and Giscard d'Estaing. Beneath the surface, however, the divisions go deep. The S.P.D. is not a socialist party in any sense which would have been understood by Sidney Webb or R. H. Tawney, let alone by Karl Marx. The vast majority of its members are solidly committed to the 'social market economy', and it is more hostile to *dirigiste* economic policies than are either the French Gaullists or the British Conservatives. The French Socialist party professes a rather eclectic form of Marxism, and fought the last two elections in uneasy alliance with the Communists; in its rhetoric, at any rate, it stands for the complete transformation of society. As everyone knows, the British Labour Party is an alliance of two bitterly hostile factions, whose policies and aims are not merely different but logically incompatible, and which hang together only because they know that the alternative is to hang separately.

It is true that these differences conceal certain fundamental similarities. In nearly all Community countries, politics revolve around what the American political sociologist, Seymour Martin Lipset, once called the 'democratic class struggle'.[4] Of course, the struggle takes different forms in different countries. In prosperous Northern Europe, where the goals of welfare-state social democracy have largely been achieved, much of the old passion has gone out of it, and the concrete policy differences between 'working class' and 'bourgeois' parties are so small as to be almost invisible. In Italy, where these goals have not been achieved, and in France, where they have been achieved only partially, the struggle is much fiercer. Britain, with an advanced welfare state but an unproductive economy, falls somewhere between North and South. There are other complicating factors too. In Italy, the Communists are the 'working-class' party, not the Socialists; thus, the Communists are free to follow a moderate line, designed to win over the middle ground, without fearing that they may lose their working-class base as a result. In France, Socialists and Communists both lay claim to the proletarian mantle, with the result that each is reluctant to move too far to the centre, for fear that the other may outbid it on the left. In both Italy and France, moreover, older cleavages — that between clerical and anti-clerical, for example, and in France perhaps even that between 'Republican' and 'anti-Republican' — still have some kick left in them; partly because of this, the right-wing parties in Italy and France are not straightforwardly 'bourgeois' parties on the North European Model. In Ireland, a pre-industrial society only now emerging from a semi-colonial status, the 'democratic class struggle' has little relevance to politics; in Belgium, it has been overlaid by ethnic conflicts.

When all the necessary qualifications have been made, however, the fact remains that in seven out of the nine Member States of the Community it still makes sense to describe politics in terms of a struggle between left and right, and to describe that struggle in terms of a distributional conflict between working-class parties and non-working-class parties. And that, of course, is the logic of the trans-national party federations we have been discussing, and of the group structure of the European Parliament. The Socialist parties represented in the European Parliament have different policies and different ideologies, which reflect the special peculiarities of the societies in which they operate. On some issues some of them may advocate policies which in other countries would be advocated by the 'right' rather than by the 'left'. Each of them, however, falls squarely on the 'left', 'working-class' side of its own national dividing line. That is what holds the group together, in spite of the ideological differences between its member parties; and that is why its members recognise each other, sometimes with a start of surprise, as brothers beneath the skin. The non-Socialist groups do not fit this pattern quite so easily because the non-Socialist parties in the Member States do not fit the equivalent national patterns quite so easily. Even so, they at least have in common the fact that they are not Socialist.

The paradox is that this is a national, not a Community, logic; and that, in spite of the differences between the national parties that belong to them, the party groups in the European Parliament are in fact held together by national, not by Community, ties. The French and German Socialists follow very different policies at the national level. Yet the reason they both belong to the Socialist group is that their national positions are sufficiently similar for them to speak roughly the same political language and to see themselves as distantly related members of the same political family. Unfortunately, however, this national logic — the distributional logic of Professor Lipset's 'democratic class struggle' — has little or no bearing on the questions which have to be decided at Community level. Distributional battles are fought at Community level, of course, but the antagonists are the rich and poor Member States, not rich and poor social classes. Most Community issues are hardly distributional at all, and cannot sensibly be discussed in the 'right-left' terminology of national politics. This, of course, is why the divisions in the Commission cut across party lines. On the hard, practical questions which face Commissioners week by week — questions such as energy policy, industrial policy, competition policy, fishing policy, agricultural prices, the attitude to be adopted to low-cost imports from Asia and South America, even monetary union and the steps necessary to attain it — the parties *qua* parties have nothing to say. What is the proper Socialist attitude towards fishing quotas? What should Christian Democrats think about nuclear power? Can there be a distinctively Liberal aero-space policy? The answers to these questions are, of course, 'none', 'nothing' and 'no'. Yet these are the issues which face Community decision makers and about which the elected Parliament will have to make up its mind.

That is only the beginning of the story. Traditional politicians, whose lives have been spent waging the 'democratic class struggle', are apt to imagine that questions to which that struggle is irrelevant are not really political questions at all:

that the only questions to which it is possible to give a prin-
cipled, *political* answer are questions which can be discussed in
the traditional language of 'left' and 'right': that because the
only logic they know is the logic of 'left' and 'right' no other
political logic exists. Politicians of this school tend to see the
issues facing the Community as discrete, technical problems,
requiring *ad hoc* technical solutions. In reality, almost all the
practical problems facing the Community raise, in one form or
another, the same fundamental question, should the Community become more supranational or not? That question cannot be discussed meaningfully in the language of 'left' and
'right', but it is nevertheless a highly political question which
can only be answered in terms of a political principle and a
political logic. The dividing line which really matters in Community politics is the line between those who believe that the
Community should become more supranational and those who
believe that it should remain an association of sovereign national
states. And the line that divides nationalists from supranationalists cuts right across the line that divides Socialists from
anti-Socialists.

The Dutch Labour party, the Belgian Socialist parties, both
Italian Socialist parties and, perhaps less emphatically, the
German Social Democratic party all fall on the supranationalist
side of the nationalist-supranationalist dividing line. The British
Labour Party, the Danish Social Democratic party and (a little
less certainly) the French Socialist party and the Irish Labour
Party fall on the nationalist side. The French Republicans
probably, though not certainly, fall on the nationalist side too.
Otherwise, the Liberal and Christian Democratic parties all
fall, with different degrees of emphasis, on the supranationalist
side. The French Communists fall heavily on the nationalist
side; the Italian Communists slightly less heavily on the supranationalist side. Though the present leadership of the
British Conservative party has taken a rather nationalistic
line, the Conservative group in the European Parliament are
mostly supranationalists; and the odds are that the directly
elected Conservative Members will also follow a more supranational line in practice than that taken by the party leadership
at home. The French Gaullists, on the other hand, clearly fall

hard on the nationalist side of the line, and will continue to do so in almost all conceivable circumstances.

Towards a new Community System

The implications are clear. The Community's embryonic party system is an artificial construct, which reflects national rather than Community realities. It has taken its present form partly because most Members of the European Parliament have been national politicians first, and European politicians only second; partly because the European Parliament has played such a small part in the Community's decision-making process that the artificiality of the present group structure has not become apparent; and partly, no doubt, because the national parties would have fought hard against the emergence of a different structure, which would necessarily have cut across national lines. The more power Parliament acquires, however, the clearer it will be that the present group divisions are irrelevant to the issues on which its Members have to vote, and the more likely they are to group themselves in a different way. The present trans-national federations and party groups do not, in short, provide an appropriate basis for the party system which would be needed in a parliamentary Europe. If such a Europe is to come into existence, the party Europe which is its concomitant will have to take a different form.

That does not mean, however, that a party Europe is impossible, though it probably does mean that it will emerge only gradually and messily, with a lot of backward glances on the part of those concerned. Most national party systems are, after all, much more brittle than they look. The three great political families of Western Europe — the Socialists, the Liberals and the Christian Democrats — all draw their inspiration, however distantly, from political theories first formulated in response to the Industrial Revolution. Socialism, liberalism and social catholicism were the products of the psychological and social crisis experienced by traditional, pre-industrial societies when the new industrial civilisation of the nineteenth century spread across Europe. Inevitably, they have become less and less relevant to the practical problems which their adherents face in governing the mature industrial societies of today. The parties based on them survive because they are established machines, with organised adherents, ancient memories and stirring battle cries. But the adherents are dying off and their memories with them, while the battle cries sound less and less convincing to a new generation. Even at the national level, at any rate in the welfare states of northern Europe, the old distributional struggle has lost much of its edge while the old dividing line between 'left' and 'right' has almost ceased to be an accurate guide to governmental conduct. That, of course, is why the Governments formed by the traditional parties operate piecemeal and *ad hoc*, responding to the buffetings of circumstances instead of trying to master events. It is also why non-class parties like the Scottish and Welsh Nationalists in the United Kingdom and the Progress Party in Denmark have been able, given appropriate circumstances, to make such rapid headway. Some of the established national parties will probably try to prevent the emergence of a Communist party system grouped around the nationalist-supranationalist dividing line, and for the reasons already given the directly elected Members are likely to be fairly responsive to national party pressures immediately after they are elected. But in the long run the pressure of events is likely to prove stronger than the pressure of the national parties.

It is not likely that a nationalist-supranationalist system will come into being quickly or tidily. For a long time it and the existing 'left–right' system will probably overlap in a puzzling and superficially illogical way. But it would be a mistake to make too much of this. What is under discussion, after all, is the possible emergence of a system appropriate to a continent. Analogies with the systems of the centralised, medium-sized, nation states that make up the Community are bound to be misleading. The right analogy is with the United States, and with the United States at a fairly early period in its history. The American Whigs and Democrats in the 1830s and 1840s were loose coalitions of state parties, which usually operated at the state level, but which came together once every four years to contest presidential elections. They were held together, to the

extent that they were held together at all, by their views on
federal questions. Their views on state questions were often not
merely different, but opposed. The same was true even of the
Republican and Democratic parties in the late nineteenth and
early twentieth centuries. The distributional battles of late nineteenth and early twentieth century America were fought out
inside the parties, not between them. It was not until the New
Deal of the 1930s — if then — that the two great American
parties could meaningfully be categorised in terms of a division
between left and right or between liberalism and conservatism.

Looked at against this background, the divisions within the
nationalist and supranationalist camps in present-day Europe
are neither particularly surprising nor particularly deep. If
they come into formal existence, they will be coalitions of
national parties. They will be divided at the national level
though united at the Community level: so were their American
counterparts in the days of Andrew Jackson and Martin Van
Buren. The Members returned under their banners, if and when
they contest elections in their own right, will not always vote
on party lines: nor did American Whig and Democratic
Congressmen in the 1830s and 1840s. Sometimes, they will
vote on national lines instead: in exactly the same way,
American Whig and Democratic Congressmen often voted on
state lines.

The American analogy should not be pushed too far. The
nineteenth-century Whigs and Democrats had to mobilise the
political energies of a thinly settled, newly colonised continent,
with few established traditions or structures. They did not have
to overcome the opposition of deep-rooted party machines or
to persuade voters to ignore deep-rooted party loyalties. Moreover, they operated under a presidential constitution, and it is
at least arguable that they would never have come into existence
if they had not had to fight presidential elections across the
whole country, once every four years. Yet, for the reasons
discussed in Chapter 4 of this book, the Community is unlikely
to acquire a presidential system in the foreseeable future.
Because of all this, it would be a mistake to expect European
nationalists and supranationalists to take exactly the same path
as the American Whigs and Democrats took. We are not likely

to see nationalist and supranationalist party conventions. Candidates for the European Parliament will probably continue to fight elections under the existing national labels for a long time to come. The Members may continue to belong to the existing party groups once they have been elected. But it does not follow that, because the nationalist and supranationalist tendencies discussed here are unlikely to be expressed by tight-knit, highly organised political parties on the conventional West European model, they will have no political reality at all. The American analogy is a reminder that Europe is, after all, a continent, not a nation state, and that the politics of a continent are almost certain to be organised differently from the politics of a nation state. What matters is that the division between nationalists and supranationalists should be clear, that those on either side of the dividing line should formulate coherent policies and stand by their policies thereafter, and that the electorate should be able to choose between them. To assume that this can only be achieved by tight-knit machines, organised in the way that national parties in the Member States of the Community are currently organised, is to allow oneself to be blinkered by the past. The founding fathers of the Community were prepared to break intellectually with the national model when they set it up. There is no reason why the politicians whose task it is to democratise the structure which the founding fathers bequeathed to us should be less imaginative.

A supranationalist group might emerge quite quickly. The supranationalists outnumber the nationalists, and have more in common with each other than the nationalists have. The supranationalist camp contains almost all parties of the democratic centre – the Christian Democrats, the Social Democrats of prosperous Northern Europe, most of the Liberals, the moderate, consensual wing of the British Conservative Party. Even the British Labour Party is not totally without supranationalists, though at the time of writing it does not look as though many of them will get to Strasbourg under their proper colours. Opposing them will be the atavistic right and the more conservative class warriors of the left — the French Gaullists, the French Communists, the left and 'old' right of the British

Labour Party. Welding the supranationalists together, and keeping them together in the face of contrary pressures from national governments and national parties, will require political skills of a high order. It would be unnecessarily pessimistic to assume that such skills cannot be forthcoming.

All this will, however, pose a formidable challenge to the Commission and an even more formidable challenge to the Community's electors. Since the middle 1960s, at any rate, the Commission has given a far higher priority to its dialogue with the Council than to its relationship with Parliament. It has courted ministers and heads of government, and trembled at the prospect of their wrath. It has taken Parliament for granted, and treated it with a mixture of condescension and indifference. If the perspectives sketched out here are to be realised, it will have to reverse its priorities. It will have to be prepared to damage its standing in the national capitals for the sake of parliamentary support; Commissioners will have to put attendance at parliamentary debates ahead of close encounters with foreign ministers; Commission officials will have to recognise that the institution draws its authority from Parliament and counts for nothing without Parliament. An even heavier responsibility lies with the voters, and with the media which have to interpret the election campaign for them. The traditional national parties will have a strong incentive to fudge the issues, to pretend that the European election is only a national election writ small, to concentrate on mobilising their traditional voters by playing their traditional tunes. If direct elections are to move the Community forward, the electors of Europe will have to make it clear that they are not prepared to be mobilised in that way: that they, at any rate, recognise that Community issues are different from national issues and have to be approached in a different fashion: in short, that they are adults and expect their future representatives to treat them as adults.

Appendix

European Parties and National Parties

The Party Groups

There are six party groups in the European Parliament—the Communists and Allies, the Socialists, the Christian Democrats, the European Progressive Democrats ('Gaullists') and the Liberals and Democrats. In addition, there are three Independent members. The chart below shows the strength of the Groups in late 1978 and their order of seating in the hemicycle.

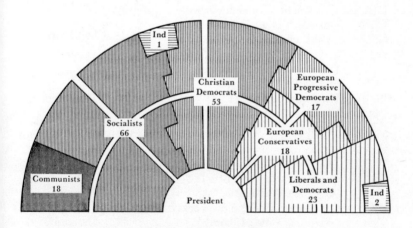

The political groups

Parliament sits in political groups, not in national delegations:
Communists on the left, Liberals on the right.

(Source: European Parliament Information Office, London)

129

APPENDIX

In October 1978 these groups included representatives of the following 48 national parties:

SOCIALIST GROUP

BSP	Belgische Socialistische Partij	Belgium
PSB	Parti socialiste belge	
S	Socialdemokratiet	Denmark
PS	Parti socialiste	France
RG	Mouvement des Radicaux de gauche	
SPD	Sozialdemokratische Partei Deutschlands	Germany
Lab	Labour Party	Ireland
PSI	Partito socialista italiano	Italy
PSDI	Partito socialista democratico italiano	
POSL	Parti ouvrier socialiste luxembourgeois	Luxembourg
PvdA	Partij van de Arbeid	Netherlands
Lab	Labour Party	U.K.

CHRISTIAN-DEMOCRATIC GROUP

CUP	Christelijke Volkspartij	Belgium
PSC	Parti social-chrétien	
RDS	Réformateurs et démocrates sociaux	France
UCDP	Union centriste des démocrates de progrès	
CDU	Christlich-Demokratische Union	Germany
CSU	Christlich-Soziale Union	
FG	Fine Gael Party	Ireland
DC	Democrazia Cristiana	Italy
SVP	Südtiroler Volkspartei	
PCS	Parti chrétien social	Luxembourg
CDA	Christen Democratisch Appel	Netherlands
KP	Katholieke Volkspartij	

LIBERAL AND DEMOCRATIC GROUP

PRLW	Parti des réformes et de la liberté de Wallonie	Belgium
PVV	Partij voor Vrijheid en Vooruitgang	
V	Venstre (Danish Liberals)	Denmark
PR	Parti républicain	France
RIAS	Républicains indépendants d'action sociale	
UDF	Union pour la Démocratie Française	
FDP	Freie Demokratische Partei	Germany

130

PLI	Partito liberale italiano	Italy
PRI	Partito Repubblicano italiano	
PD	Parti démocratique	Luxembourg
VVD	Volkpartij voor Vrijheid en Democratie	Netherlands
Lib	Liberal Party	U.K.

EUROPEAN CONSERVATIVE GROUP

CD	Centrum-Demokraterue	Denmark
KF	Det Konservative folksparti	
Cons	Conservative and Unionist Party	U.K.

COMMUNIST AND ALLIES GROUP

SF	Socialistik folkeparti	Denmark
PCF	Parti communiste français	France
Ind Sin	Independente di Sinistra	Italy
PCI	Partito communista italiano	

GROUP OF EUROPEAN PROGRESSIVE DEMOCRATS

FRP	Fremskridtspartiet	Denmark
RPR	Rassemblement pour la République	France
FF	Fianna Fail Party	Ireland

NON-ATTACHED

| DN | Democrazia nationale | Italy |
| SNP | Scottish National Party | U.K. |

The Transnational Party Federations

The three transnational federations referred to in the text are the Confederation of Socialist Parties of the European Community (founded in April 1974), the Federation of Liberal and Democratic Parties (founded in March 1976) and the European People's Party (founded in April 1976). At the time of their respective foundations, they included the following national parties:

CONFEDERATION OF SOCIALIST PARTIES IN THE EUROPEAN COMMUNITY

Parti socialiste belge/Belgische socialistische partij (PSB/BSP)
Socialdemokratiet (S), Denmark
Sozialdemokratische Partei Deutschlands (SPD)
Parti socialiste de France (PS)
Partito socialista democratico italiano (PSDI)

APPENDIX

Partito socialista italiano (PSI)
Irish Labour Party
Parti ouvrier socialiste luxembourgeois (PSOL)
Partij van de Arbeid (PvdA), Netherlands
British Labour Party

FEDERATION OF LIBERAL AND DEMOCRATIC PARTIES IN THE EUROPEAN
COMMUNITIES

Parti libéral (PL), Belgium
Parti des réformes et de la liberté wallon (PRLW), Belgium
Partij voor Vrijheid en Vooruitgang (PVV), Belgium
Det Radikale Venstre, Denmark
Venstres Landsorganisation, Denmark
Freie Demokratische Partei (FDP), Germany
Mouvement des Radicaux de gauche, France
Parti radical socialiste (PRS), France
Républicans indépendants (RI), France
Partito liberale (PL), Italy
Partito Repubblicano italiano (PRI), Italy
Parti démocratique (PD), Luxembourg
Volkspartij voor vrijheid en democratie (VVD), Netherlands
The Liberal Party Organization, United Kingdom

EUROPEAN PEOPLE'S PARTY

Christelijke Volkspartij (CVP) and Parti social-chrétien (PSC),
Belgium
Christlich-Demokratische Union (CDU) and Christlich-Soziale
Union (CSU), Germany
Centre des démocrates sociaux (CDS) France
Democrazia Cristiana (DC), Italy
Südtiroler Volkspartei (SVP), Italy
Fine Gael, Ireland
Parti chrétien social (PCS), Luxembourg
Antirevolutionaire Partij (ARP), Netherlands
Christelijk Historische Unie (CHU), Netherlands
Katholieke Volkspartij (KVP), Netherlands

(Source: Tenth *General Report on the Activities of the European Communities*, 1977.)

Notes

Chapter 1 Pragmatism is not Enough

1   Valentine Herman and Juliet Lodge, 'Is the European Parliament a Parliament?', *European Journal of Political Research*, 6 (1978), pp. 157–80.

2   'Nous ne coalisons pas des états, nous unissons des hommes'; epigraph of Jean Monnet's *Mémoires*, Fayard, 1976. English translation: *Memoirs*, Collins, 1978.

3   Edward Heath, *Old World, New Horizons, Britain, the Common Market and the Atlantic Alliance*, Oxford University Press, 1970, p. 57.

4   For the view that the British genius is inherently different from those of her continental neighbours see Paul Johnson, *Offshore Islanders*, Weidenfeld & Nicolson, 1972; for the view that membership of the Community is incompatible with parliamentary sovereignty see any number of speeches by Enoch Powell, notably his speech in the House of Commons debate on the principle of entry in October 1971 (*Hansard*, vol. 823, cols. 2184–9); for characteristic expressions of the left-wing view that true internationalism lay in opposing entry see the speeches of Joan Lestor, Eric Deakins and Barbara Castle in the same debate (ibid., cols. 952–7, 1643–9 and 1837–49).

5   See Michael Howard, *The British Way in Warfare: A Reappraisal* (Neale lecture in English history, 1974).

6   Harold Macmillan, *Pointing The Way, 1959–61*, Macmillan, 1972, pp. 54–5.

7   Harold Wilson, *The Labour Government 1964–1970, A Personal Record*, Weidenfeld & Nicolson/Michael Joseph, 1971, pp. 687–8.

8   Address to Brussels Labour Group, February 6, 1978.

9   Quoted in Uwe Kitzinger, *Diplomacy and Persuasion*, Thames and Hudson, 1973, p. 148.

10 R. H. S. Crossman, *The Diaries of a Cabinet Minister*, Hamish

Hamilton/Jonathan Cape, 1976, vol. II, pp. 81–2.

11 See the complaints by W. T. Rodgers, one of the most committed pro-Europeans in British politics, about 'the problems and surprises' which membership of the Community has brought to Britain, and about the 'pin pricks' which come from Brussels. (*Hansard*, May 3, 1978, vol. 949, cols. 228–9.)

12 John Pinder, 'Positive Integration and Negative Integration, some problems of economic union in the E.E.C.', *The World Today*, vol. 24, pp. 88–110.

13 By Andrew Shonfield, *Europe: Journey To an Unknown Destination*, Allen Lane/Penguin, 1973.

14 *Report of the Working Party examining the Problem of the Enlargement of the Powers of the European Parliament. Bulletin* of the European Communities, Supplement 4/72, pp. 25–7.

Chapter 2 Forward or Back

1 Though Mr Papandreou's Panhellenic Socialist Movement opposes Greek entry into the Community on grounds reminiscent of those advanced by the left wing of the British Labour Party in the early 1970s.

2 L. Tsoukalis, 'A Community of Twelve in Search of an Identity', *International Affairs*, July 1978.

3 *Economic and Sectoral Aspects: Commission analyses supplementing its views on enlargement.* COM (78) 200. Unless otherwise stated, figures on the economic implications of enlargement are quoted from here.

4 Figures from COM (78) 102 final, COM (78) 103 final and COM (78) 529 final.

5 *The Economic Situation in the Community.* COM (77) 640 final.

6 Rt Hon. R. Jenkins at the opening ceremony of the XIth Federal Congress, Deutsches Gewerkschaftbund, Hamburg, May 21, 1978.

7 COM (78) 529 final.

8 Private information.

9 'The Views and Positions of the Social Partners on Trade Liberalisation and Protectionism'. Study by the Social Partners' Bureau of the Commission, 1978.

10 The best discussion of the implications of enlargement for majority voting is contained in the Commission paper, *The Transitional Period and the Institutional Implications of Enlargement*, COM (78) 190 final.

11 *Report of the Study Group on the Role of Public Finance in European*

Integration, Commission of the European Communities, April 1977, vol. I.

Chapter 3 *The Institutional Imbalance*

1   For two stimulating discussions of the implications of regionalism for the Community see Roderick MacFarquhar, 'The Community, the Nation State and the Regions', and Tom Ellis, 'Why A Federal Britain?' in Bernard Burrows, Geoffrey Denton and Geoffrey Edwards (eds) *Federal Solutions to European Issues,* Macmillan, 1978.

2   See Eugen Weber, *Peasants Into Frenchmen, The Modernization of Rural France 1870–1914,* Chatto, 1977, especially part II, 'The Agencies of Change'.

3   Percentage of respondents saying that their countries' membership of the Community is 'a good thing' in the original six Member States:

	Autumn 1973	Autumn 1975	Autumn 1977	Spring 1978
Belgium	57	59	60	58
France	61	67	57	54
Germany	63	61	59	58
Holland	63	67	74	78
Italy	69	75	70	65
Luxembourg	67	78	73	73

(Source: *Euro-Baromètre* no. 9, July 1978.)

4   For an interesting discussion of the tensions between national and Community officials see Luxemburgensis, 'The Emergence of a European Sovereignty' in G. Ionescu (ed.) *Between Sovereignty and Integration,* Croom Helm, 1974, pp. 118–34.

5   Jean Monnet, *Mémoires,* Fayard, 1976, pp. 270–4.

6   See in particular the excellent discussion in David Coombes, *Politics and Bureaucracy in the European Community,* Allen & Unwin, 1970, esp. chapters 11–13.

Chapter 4 *Direct Elections: Opportunities and Dangers*

1   J. Fitzmaurice, 'National Parliaments and European Policy Making: the case of Denmark', *Parliamentary Affairs,* vol. XXIX, no. 3, summer 1976.

2 The only other Community country in which there is pressure to follow the Danish example is Britain. But no British Government has ever granted a House of Commons committee powers remotely comparable to those of the Folketing's Market Relations Committee, and it is almost inconceivable that any British Government ever would.

3 The following table shows how the European Parliament's work has increased over the last years:

No. of	1975	1976	1977
Resolutions	244	262	256
Committee Meetings	271	295	311
Written Questions	876	973	1,209
Oral Questions	79	107	84

(Source: Tenth and Eleventh *General Reports on the Activities of the European Communities*, published in 1977 and 1978.

4 See S. M. Lipset, *The First New Nation*, Heinemann, 1964, especially Part I, for a stimulating discussion of these issues.

5 Quoted in Valentine Herman and Juliet Lodge, *The European Parliament and the European Community*, 1978, p. 75.

6 Commissioners' excuses for failing to attend part-sessions of the Parliament range from the predictable (important trips in distant continents) to the bizarre (a dentist's appointment in Düsseldorf). Even more remarkable than the Commission's unwillingness to take its parliamentary responsibilities seriously, however, is Parliament's willingness to allow itself to be treated in this way.

7 Sir Peter Kirk in the European Parliament, June 14, 1976. Quoted in Herman and Lodge, op. cit., p. 51.

8 Robert Jackson, *The Powers of the European Parliament*, Conservative Group for Europe, 1977, p. 38.

Chapter 5 A Parliamentary Europe

1 The Vedel Report, chapter IV, pp. 36–49.

2 *Draft Report on the Powers of the European Parliament*, PE 37 065/rev., especially chapters I to III.

3 The 'concertation procedure', introduced in 1975, applies only to proposed Community acts with financial implications. Under it, when differences of opinion occur between Council and

Parliament, a 'conciliation committee' comprising representatives of the Council, Parliament and Commission is set up. If the committee decides that agreement between Council and Commission is probable, the proposal is re-submitted to Parliament for a second Opinion. The Council has the last word.

4　Herman and Lodge, *The European Parliament and the European Community*, pp. 34–41.

5　Robert Jackson, *The Powers of the European Parliament*, pp. 18–25.

6　See *Scrutiny of Public Expenditure and Administration*, First Report from the Select Committee on Procedure (Session 1968–9), July 1969.

7　Op. cit., pp. 45–59.

8　Op. cit., chapter IV.

9　Op. cit., p. 67.

10　*Report to the Council and the Commission on the Realisation by Stages of Economic and Monetary Union in the Community*, supplement to *Bulletin* 11, 1970, pp. 12–13.

11　M. O'Donoghue, 'Budgetary Powers of the European Parliament', in vol. II of *Report of the Study Group on the Role of Public Finance in European Integration*, April 1977, pp. 564–72.

12　Official Journal of the European Communities, *Debates of the European Parliament*, January 1978, no. 225, p. 63.

13　In 1976 Parliament gave Opinions on 246 Commission proposals. It suggested modifications in 61 cases. The Commission accepted 32 of these modifications (52 per cent). In the first eleven months of 1977 Parliament gave 273 Opinions on Commission proposals. It suggested modifications in 44 cases. The Commission accepted 30 of its modifications (68 per cent). (Figures prepared by the Secretariat-General of the Commission in December 1977.)

Chapter 6　A Party Europe?

1　'I shall ... need to be a coalition rather than a partisan President. I shall be a partisan only for Europe.' Rt Hon. R. Jenkins, inaugural address to the European Parliament, January 1977. *Official Journal of the European Communities, Debates of the European Parliament*, no. 211, January 1977, p. 15.

2　J. Fitzmaurice, *Party Groups in the European Parliament*, Saxon House, 1975, p. 171.

3　Ibid., pp. 169–70.

4　S. M. Lipset, *Political Man*, Heinemann, 1963, p. 220.

Note on Further Reading

An exhaustive bibliography, even confined to the topics covered in this book, would run to enormous length; what follows is merely a select list of the published material which I have found particularly useful or stimulating.

1 General Surveys

WALTER HALLSTEIN, *Europe in the Making*, English translation, Allen & Unwin, 1972. By the first President of the E.E.C. Commission.
UWE KITZINGER, *The Challenge of the Common Market*, Blackwell, 1962.
ROY PRYCE, *The Politics of the European Community*, Butterworth, 1973.

2 Historical

M. CAMPS, *Britain and the European Community, 1955–1963*, Oxford University Press, 1964.
—— *European Unification in the Sixties*, Oxford University Press, 1967.
UWE KITZINGER, *Diplomacy and Persuasion*, Thames and Hudson, 1973.
R. MAYNE, *The Recovery of Europe*, Weidenfeld & Nicolson, 1970.
JEAN MONNET, *Memoirs*, Collins, 1978. (In French, *Mémoires*, Fayard, 1976.)
R. MORGAN, *West European Integration Since 1945: The Shaping of the European Community*, Batsford, 1972.
F. R. WILLIS, *France, Germany, and the New Europe, 1945–1967*, 2nd ed., Oxford University Press, 1968.

3 Institutional and Policy Questions

B. BURROWS, G. DENTON and G. EDWARDS, *Federal Solutions to European Issues*, Macmillan, 1978.

D. COOMBES, *Politics and Bureaucracy in the European Community*, Allen & Unwin, 1970.

J-F. DENIAN, *L'Europe Interdite*, Paris, 1977.

V. HERMAN and J. LODGE, *The European Parliament and the European Community*, Macmillan, 1978.

G. IONESCU (ed.), *Between Sovereignty and Integration*, Croom Helm, 1974.

—— (ed.), *The New Politics of European Integration*, Macmillan, 1972.

R. JACKSON, *The Powers of the European Parliament*, Conservative Group for Europe, 1977.

M. KOHNSTAMM and W. HAGER (eds), *Nation Writ Large? Foreign-Policy Problems before the European Community*, Macmillan, 1973.

A. SHONFIELD, *Europe: Journey to an Unknown Destination*, Allen Lane/Penguin, 1973.

H. THOMAS, *Europe the Radical Challenge*, Quartet Books, 1973.

L. TSOUKALIS, *The Politics and Economics of European Monetary Integration*, Allen & Unwin, 1977.

H. WALLACE, W. WALLACE and C. WEBB, *Policy-Making in the European Communities*, Wiley, 1977.

4 Official Reports and Statements

R. JENKINS, *Europe's Present Challenge and Future Opportunity*, Jean Monnet Lecture, Florence, 1977.

The Enlargement of the Community, 17th Reprint, House of Lords Select Committee on the European Communities, H.M.S.O., 1978.

Report to the Council and the Commission on the Realisation by Stages of Economic and Monetary Union (Werner Report). Supplement to *Bulletin* 11, 1970.

Report of the Study Group on the Role of Public Finance in European Integration (MacDougall Report). Commission of the European Communities, April 1977.

Report of the Working Party examining the Problem of the Powers of the European Parliament (Vedel Report). Supplement to *Bulletin* 4, 1972.

Index

welfare state, 120–1, 125
Welsh Nationalists, 125
Werner Plan, 45, 46, 103, 104
'Western Summit', 21

Wilson, Harold, 9, 10, 12–13, 80, 116

Yom Kippur War (1973), 45–6